The life and teaching of
PACHOMIUS

WELLSPRINGS OF FAITH is a selection from the writings by Christians from the earliest times. The choice of texts introduces the reader to a range of the most notable and beautiful literature of the Christian tradition, a literature which can help Christians to deepen their faith and life of prayer.

This series Wellsprings of Faith (formerly Witnesses for Christ) is a project sponsored by A.I.M (Aide Inter-Monastères), an international organisation to serve the needs of young monastic communities in Africa and Asia. By providing patristic and monastic literature in an easily readable form, it hopes also to be of use to people throughout the English-speaking world.

Acknowledgments and thanks are due to a team of volunteer translators and others who have given their services.

WELLSPRINGS OF FAITH

vol xiii

The Life and Teaching of

PACHOMIUS

First published in 1998

Gracewing	in conjunction with	The Secretariat of
Fowler Wright Books		Aide Inter - Monastères
2 Southern Avenue Leominster		7 Rue d'Îssy
Herefordshire		92170 Vanves
HR6 OQF		France

put into English by	revised from the Coptic and Greek by
Sr Mary Dominique OC Slough	Br A Marett-Crosby OSB
and D.Mary Groves OSB	Ampleforth Abbey

Text Sources :
Bohairic Life 1-127
Ist Greek Life and Sahidic Life - extracts
Corpus Scriptorum Christianorum Orientalium vol 160

ISBN   0 85244 416 8

Typesetting by Kylemore Abbey
Connemara
County Galway

Printed by
Redwood Books, Trowbridge, Wiltshire BA14 8RN

Introduction to the Life of Pachomius

Pachomius was born during the reign of the Emperor Diocletian, the son of pagan parents who lived in rural Egypt, the Thebaîd. He seems never to have met the Christian people of that region for he did not hear of the faith until AD 312 when he was a prisoner during a civil war in Egypt. Pachomius had been forced to become a soldier in that war and, while in prison after being captured, he saw some people bringing food to the prisoners. This amazed him and when he was told that these were Christians, who were 'kind to everyone, including strangers', he learnt of their beliefs and was baptised. Some of the stories of his life record that he became a monk at once, but it probably took him a little time to discover his vocation. He spent some years living in a little community and serving the people, and only after this experience did he decide to seek God as a monk.

He went to live with a great monk called Palamon, following his teaching as St Antony had done with his spiritual father forty years before, and together they moved to a deserted village at Tabennesi where they built a monastery. After Palamon died, Pachomius' own brother, John, joined him but this first community was very difficult for Pachomius, and some of his followers were so difficult that after spending time in prayer he chased them away from the monastery. But others who came were men who wanted to be true disciples and gradually the community grew from its humble beginnings into a great monastery.

One story says that Pachomius led three thousand monks, and while we do not know if this is quite correct we do know that he was able to found many other monasteries, at Phbow (which became his own monastery), Seneset, and Thbew, In his lifetime it seems that his teaching was of great importance to all the monks, who gathered every evening to hear it, and as the monasteries expanded it became important to write that teaching down, so that it could be explained to novices and to those who lived away from Pachomius.

He had many assistants, of whom the greatest was Theodore, and these men led the other communities, while always looking to Pachomius for their inspiration. As he was dying he entrusted the care of the monasteries to Horsiesios, who had known Pachomius for many years, and Horsiesios worked to preserve the rules that Pachomius had laid down, rules which described the daily routine of work and prayer, the order of the community, and the duties of a senior. Later, lives of Pachomius were written to keep his memory alive, and some of these writings were taken to Rome and preserved in Lain. From there they influenced monastic development in the West.

Lots of monks wrote lives of their father Pachomius in the years after his death. Some wrote short stories of what he had done or said, and some wrote whole biographies. They are all written in different languages. The two most important lives which have survived are in Greek (G^1) and in a dialect of Coptic called Bohairic (Bo). These two lives are probably based on the same original life, which did not survive, and the authors selected what they wanted to remember from that original life. Our text is mostly from Bo, though some stories come from G^1 and a few from a very early account in another Coptic dialect called Sahidic (S^1), which records some other traditions about Pachomius.

There are many examples in the Lives of Pachomius of his teaching to his community : often they are based on Scripture and we are told that 'some who loved him very much wrote down how he explainedthe Scriptures'. At other times he spoke on particular problemsinmonastic life, teaching the monks the value of humility, purity of life,simplicity, and forgiveness of each other. We give the text of one such teaching.

The reason for the sermon is that a monk has not forgiven another monk and so Pachomius teaches the whole community how they should live together as a community. Pachomius was the first of the monks of Egypt to try to live in a close community and so he very much needed to show how this was to be done, calling on the monks to live like the great saints in the Bible, to persevere, and to follow the teachings of Christ, using Scripture to explain how this was to be done. A lot of this teaching is also found in other monastic fathers, especially St Athanasius, who knew Pachomius and whose sermons have many of the same ideas in them, but Pachomius writes from inside the community, and we know that he knew his monks very well. One story in the Lives tells us how Pachomius, visiting one of his monasteries, was asked to give the monks some teaching to help them in their own monastic lives, and it is probably from just such an event that the 'Monk with a Grudge' comes. Texts like this one remind us also of the wisdom of St Benedict, for it is from this tradition that he drew much of his teaching.

Br Anthony Marett-Crosby OSB

Feast of St Antony the Abbot
January 17th 1998

LIFE OF PACHOMIUS

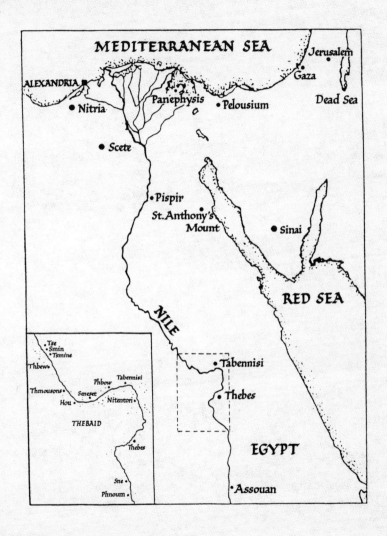

THE LIFE OF ST PACHOMIUS

PROLOGUE
THE FIRST MONKS AND THE MARTYRS

1   The Word of God who made all things
spoke to his Prophets and servants, and to all the prophets.
Then he appeared and spoke as man
and as the seed of Abraham,
for he had promised him blessing for the nations.   Gen 22.17,18
And he commanded his disciples :
'Go, teach all nations.
Baptise them, in the name of the Father
and of the Son and of the Holy Spirit.'   Mt 28.19
The good news of the Gospel spread through all the world.
But God wanted a proof of faith from Christians.
Pagan emperors made a great attack on the Christians everywhere.
They tortured many of them till they died.
The last to receive the crown of martyrdom
was Archbishop Peter of Alexandria, in Egypt.

Then the faith of the Christians greatly increased.
From that time on there began to appear
monasteries and places of ascetics
honoured for their chastity and detachment from possessions.
The first monks had seen the patient courage of the martyrs.
Therefore they revived the way of life of the prophet Elijah,
and of those about whom the Apostle said :
'Suffering, maltreated,
they wandered in the desert and the mountains,
in caves and in holes in the ground.'   Heb 11.38
These were the first monks.

They built cells and monasteries.
They lived a hard life in the fear of God.
They had before their eyes, night and day, the cross of Christ
and the sufferings of the martyrs they had seen
and wanted to imitate.

2   The life of Abba Antony
was like that of Elijah, Elisha and John the Baptist....
In Egypt and in the Thebaîd, many pagans became Christians
after the persecutions by Diocletian and Maximian. *
The Bishops led them to God
according to the teaching of the Apostles.
They produced many of the fruits of the Holy Spirit
and came to the love of Christ.

• THE CHILDHOOD OF PACHOMIUS

3   Pachomius was born in the Thebaïd, in Upper Egypt,
in the diocese of Sne....

4   His parents were not Christians.
One day they went to offer a sacrifice
to the creatures of the Nile.
The creatures saw the boy and they fled.
The pagan priest cried to the crowd :
" Chase him away. He is the enemy of the gods.
It is because of him that they will not come to the surface."
This caused pain to his parents.
On another occasion they gave the child a drink
from the pagan sacrifice, and he was violently sick.

---

*   AD 294-305 and 305-306.   Pachomius was born about the year 292.

His baptism

7   After the persecution,
Constantius the Great became emperor.
He was the first christian emperor.

But another great ruler wanted his empire,
so he made war against him.
Constantine sent messengers into all the towns
to find out big strong young men
to train them for soldiers.
Pachomius was twenty years old. He was taken away,
although he was not very strong.

The young men were taken by boat. It travelled down the Nile.
At Thebes, the capital,
they were shut up with the other soldiers in a prison.
They were very unhappy.
But in the evening, some people of the town came to visit them
to give them food and drink.
Young Pachomius asked his companions :
"Who are they ?
They do not know us. Why are they so good to us ?"
They replied :
"They are Christians.
They come with love in the name of Jesus Christ,
Son of the God of heaven and earth."

Pachomius did not sleep.. He prayed all night:
"God of heaven and of the earth, have pity on me.
If you set me free, I also will love all people.
I will serve you and I will serve them all the days of my life."

The next morning they were led out and put into the boat,
and they travelled until they came to the town of Antinoë,
where they were again kept in the prison.

8   While they were there,
Emperor Constantine won the war.
At once he ordered all the soldiers to their homes.
Pachomius went back toward the south, to the Upper Thebaïd.
He came to a little village called Sheneset.
It was a very dry place with few inhabitants.
He settled there, growing some vegetables and date palms
so as to feed himself and any poor person or passing stranger.
After he had spent a while there
he was brought to the church and baptised.

His vocation

On the night of his baptism he had a dream.
The dew from heaven came down on his head.
It became a honey-comb in his right hand
and the honey spread over all the earth.
A voice said to him :
"Understand, Pachomius, for before long it will happen to you
as you have seen."

9   Some time later there was an infectious sickness.
This outbreak of plague caused many deaths.
Pachomius served the sick.
He carried wood to them from the forest.
He took care of their sores until they were healed.

• PACHOMIUS AND PALAMON

10   Pachomius stayed three years in that place.
A great number of people went to be with him
because he helped them.
He could not be left in peace.
So he decided to become a hermit-monk.

While he was thinking over his decision
he heard of an old hermit called Abba Palamon.
He was a great monk
who lived a little way from the village.
Pachomius left his house and vegetable garden
and the palm trees
in the charge of an old man, for the poor,
and went to visit Palamon.
He knocked on the door.
The old man looked out through the window
and said to him roughly :
"Who is it ? Why are you knocking ?"
"Father, if you please, I want to be a monk with you."
"No, you are not able. It is hard to be a monk.
Many have come and have left."
"Try me, Father, and you will know."
"It is necessary first to try yourself before you can begin.
My rule, which I learnt from my fathers, is hard.
I eat nothing until sunset all through the summer.
In winter I eat only every second or third day.
I take bread and salt without oil and without wine.
I keep watch until midnight, often all night,
to pray and to meditate on the words of God.
I also work with my hands weaving palm leaves or reeds
and whatever I earn I give to the poor."

Pachomius answered him enthusiastically :
"All that I will do. I have confidence,
with the help of God and of your prayers."
Palamon opened the door to him and he went in.
After three months he received the habit of the monks.

The two lived together a life of sacrifice and of prayer.
Together they worked making bags and mats.
They did not work for themselves but for the poor.

During the night watch,
when they felt that they wanted to sleep
they went out to carry baskets of sand from place to place
and the effort kept them awake.
In all things, Pachomius was obedient
and his patience grew, and Palamon was glad.

Penances of Palamon

11   On Easter Day, Palamon said to Pachomius :
"Today is a great feast-day
so we will prepare a midday meal."
Pachomius went to prepare the dinner.
He mixed a little oil in the salt.
Palamon saw the oil.
He clapped his hand to his forehead and said, weeping :
"My Lord was crucified and should I take some oil ?"
Pachomius threw out the salt.
"Father, I ask pardon," he said.
And the two sat down to eat bread and salt
as they did every day.

13   On the feast of the Epiphany,
when Pachomius returned from cutting trees in the forest,
on the other side of the desert,
the old man was cooking something in a pot.
Astonished, Pachomius said to himself :
'What can he be cooking on the day of Epiphany ?'
Palamon raised the cover.
There were only some green figs from the trees which they
watered each day to give fruit for the sick.
The two prayed
and they ate the green figs
and gave thanks to God.

A proud monk

14   One day, Palamon and Pachomius were seated round the fire
with a brother who lived nearby.
The brother said :
"If you have faith,
remain standing in the fire while saying the Our Father."
But Palamon recognised pride in the words he had spoken
and he said to the brother :
"Quick : your thought comes from the devil."
Taking no notice the brother went towards the glowing fire
and stood on it, reciting the prayer.
His feet were not burned.
His heart filled with pride, he returned to his cell.
Palamon said to Pachomius :
"We should not admire that man.
It is God who is permitting the demon to deceive him."
Indeed the devil knew that now the brother was in his hands.
The same night he knocked on the brother's door
in the form of a pretty woman.
The brother opened the door and the woman said to him :
"I have some debts. I am being pursued.
Let me rest here for the night."
He let her in.
But at once the devil stirred up bad desires in him
to which he consented.
Then the devil struck him to the ground
and he remained there like one dead.

Then he came weeping to Palamon and said :
"My Father, pray for me, because the devil wants to kill me.
I am the cause of my own ruin.
My pride kept me from listening to your teaching."
Pachomius and Palamon began to pray with tears
and he recovered from his distress.

But then the devil knocked him down again.
They prayed over him until he recovered and stood up.
But he took up a great log and tried to kill them.
They tried to hold him but all at once he escaped.
He ran over the mountain,
came eventually into a town fifty miles away
and there threw himself into the fire
which heated the public baths.
He was burned alive.
The old man Palamon was very sad about that wretched man
and many times he said to Pachomius :
"See what happened to that brother.
He was unable to resist the weakness of his spirit."

Pachomius' ascetical discipline

15   That story encouraged Pachomius in the fear of sin.
He learned long passages of Scripture by heart.
He made great efforts to put into practice the law of God.
He made many acts of self-denial.
He tried to be absolutely pure in heart.
He prayed alone in the desert.
When he went to the desert to gather wood
which was full of long thorns
he endured the thorns in his hands and bare feet.
He thought of the nails in the feet and hands of our Lord
when he was on the cross.

12   After four years, Pachomius again saw the dream.
The dew from heaven came down on him
and covered the surface of the whole earth.
The next evening he told the holy old man Abba Palamon.
He was quite puzzled and said :
"There is a deep meaning to explain it all.
May the Lord's will be done."

16   A short time later, Palamon fell ill
because he was old and still practised exercises of self-denial.
Older brothers from nearby brought him medicine.
For some days he obeyed them and ate food good for the sick
but he did not get well. He said:
"The martyrs had their heads and limbs cut off
or were burned to death for Christ's sake.
They endured, through faith in God.
Your food does nothing for me at all.
I will go back to my usual custom."
And he went back courageously to his former exercises.

• TABENNISI

17   One day Pachomius went into the desert
for a distance of some two kilometres
He came to an abandoned village at the side of the Nile.
It was Tabennisi.
There he began to pray for a long while.
Then he heard a voice which said to him :
"Pachomius, remain here. Build a monastery.
Young monks will come to you."
On his return he told Palamon the story.
Palamon began to weep because Pachomius,
who had been with the old man seven years,
was going to leave him.
"I believe, he said, that word comes form God.
His will be done."
They returned to Tabennisi together
and built a cell for Pachomius.
Then Palamon said to Pachomius :
"For seven years you have given me your obedience.
Now you must leave me in my old age :
it is God's will.

But we need not be entirely separated.
You will come to visit me
and then I will come to visit you,
until God comes for me."

18   A month later he fell ill again.
The brothers sent word to Pachomius.
Pachomius went back from Tabennisi to take care of him.
He remained there until the Lord came to visit Palamon.
Pachomius buried him, then he returned to Tabennisi.

Pachomius and John

19   His own brother John learned the story of Pachomius.
He travelled by boat to find him.
Pachomius was very glad.
He had not seen him since his time in the army.
Pachomius spoke the word of God to him,
and he became a monk.
They lived together.
They had nothing but the law of God.
They ate two loaves of bread daily with a little salt.
They gave the rest of what they earned by their work to the poor.
Their clothing too was very poor.
They had no more than one cloak for the two of them.
They put it on in turns to wash and dry their tunics.
For prayer they often wore a goat-hair garment.
They prayed standing erect without moving,
both hands extended, to guard against sleep.
The mosquitoes bit their hands badly.
They slept seated, without support for their backs,
where they prayed.
During work they did not avoid the burning sun.
All this they did because it is written :
If anyone wants to be my disciple
let him take up his cross and follow me.   Mt 16.24

19 One day, Pachomius wanted to make their house larger,
as a small monastery, so that crowds could be received.
He began to build a wall.
But John thought they should stay alone.
He started to destroy the wall.
Pachomius became angry and said :
"John, stop that, you fool."
John also became angry and sad.
Standing with hands extended Pachomius prayed until dawn :
"Have mercy on me, Lord,
or the devil will take me when I die.
If the enemy finds little by little a place for himself in me
he will overcome me in the end.
But I believe that if in your great mercy you will help me
I shall learn to walk the way of the saints,
for they indeed put the enemy to shame, with your help.
How will I teach those you call to this life with me
if I do not begin by exercising my patience ?"

20 One day they were throwing reeds into the river
to prepare them for their work.
Suddenly a crocodile rose up and John ran away to the shore.
He cried to his brother :
" Quick, come to the shore or the crocodile will seize you
and eat you."
Pachomius laughed and said to him :
"John, do you think the beasts are their own masters ?"
Once more the crocodile came to the surface, very close.
Pachomius filled his hands with water
and hurled it in the crocodile's face, saying :
"May the Lord condemn you never to come back here."
And the crocodile submerged.
John ran to his brother.
He kissed him on the mouth, his hands and his feet, saying :
"I am your elder brother

but now I shall call you Father
because of your great faith in the Lord."

21   Pachomius underwent many temptations.
God permitted it for his training
and so that he could teach others.
Understanding the tricks of the devil,
he used to kneel with faith and bless God,
giving thanks to Christ and putting the demons to flight.

As for John, he performed great exercises of self-denial
until the day of his death.

22   Pachomius searched to find the will of God for him.
He was alone one day on an island near Tabennisi
gathering a few reeds for the work.
During the night as he was praying as usual
an angel of the Lord appeared to him.
He said three times :
"Pachomius, Pachomius, the Lord's will is
to serve the human race
and to unite them to him."
When the angel of the Lord had gone away
Pachomius thought about what he had heard
and it brought him comfort.
He said to himself : 'This comes from God.'

First organisation of the monastery

23   The providence of God sent three men to join Pachomius :
Pentaesi, Sourous and Phoi.
They said to him :
"We want to be monks with you and serve Christ."
Pachomius said to them :
"Are you able to leave your parents

to follow the Saviour ?" Lk 14.25-26
Then he tested them.
He found that their intentions were good.
He gave them the monk's habit
and received them with joy in God's love.
He led them forward little by little in the monastic life.
He taught them above all to give up the world,
their family, and themselves.
He taught them according to the Scriptures
and they bore many fruits of the Spirit.

Pachomius wished to spare his novices all worry.
"Your work, he said, is to meditate
the psalms, all of the Scriptures, but above all the Gospels."
He said to himself : 'These are the novices.
They are not yet capable of serving others.'
And he did all the work in the monastery himself.
He looked after the few vegetables in the garden,
and prepared their food.
If anyone knocked at the door of the monastery
it was he who went to answer it.
If any of them was sick
he cared for him until he was better.
Then the novices said to him :
"Father, we are sad.
Why do you do all the work alone ?"
Pachomius answered them :
"Who yokes his donkey to a water-wheel
and forgets about it without caring
until it drops down and dies ?
The Lord well knows my tiredness.
He will again send some companions
to help us in our work."

He gave them a rule, based on Scripture.
They all lived alike.
They all wore the same sort of clothes
and had the same measure of food
and they had decent sleeping arrangements.
Even when he was not teaching them,
his example encouraged them.
They said to one another :
" We used to think all the saints were made holy
from their mothers' womb.
Sinners too can have life.
Our Father was a pagan.
So then we too and all the others can follow him
for he has clothed himself with all God's commandments."
And God called others to come and join them :
Pecos, Cornelios, Paul,
another Pachomius and John,
five hermits from the neighbourhood.

24   Then, one by one,   S[1] 10-13
fifty men came from villages further south to be hermit monks.
They constructed huts at the monastery.
Pachomius gave them a rule.
Each one must support himself,
but he gave a share to Pachomius
for food and for the visitors' room.
They all ate together
and it was Pachomius who served them.
But they were not yet ready to band together into a community.
They were insincere.
They made fun of Pachomius' humility.
When he commanded them, often they refused.
He did not punish them but bore with them with great patience.
This went on for four or five years.

Then, seeing that they were not returning to God
in spite of all his patience and endurance with them,
he sent them away.
After the departure of these brothers
the Lord sent many others who made good progress.

The Church at Tabennisi

25   Pachomius saw that a lot of people had come
to live in the new village of Tabennisi.
He and the brothers built a church for them.
On Saturday evenings they went to the church
to receive the sacraments.
As it did not have a Reader
it was Pachomius who read the lessons.
Pachomius took care of the offerings
because the people were very poor.

When the brothers numbered one hundred,
Pachomius built another church within the monastery
so that they might praise God there.
On Saturday evenings the brothers went to the village
for the Eucharist, and on Sunday morning
it was the priest who came to offer the Eucharist
at the monastery.
Among the brothers there was no priest
because Pachomius said :
" It is better not to have a desire for such honours
in our community,
or there may be envy and jealousy.
It is like a spark thrown in the straw on the threshing-floor.
If it is not put out it destroys all the harvest.
It is better to obey respectfully
the priest sent us by the Church of God."

But if a priest came to be a monk,
if he had the right intention Pachomius would accept him.
He respected his rank
but he expected him to follow the rule willingly
like all the others.

The officials of the monastery

26   Pachomius realised that the brothers must help him.
He named the more capable brothers
for the material tasks and to greet the guests.
He divided the monastery into houses
and appointed one brother to be at the head of each
with a second person to help him.

At the head of the monastery
he named a chief steward
in charge of the cooking and laying tables.
He also named another monk, with an assistant,
men on whom he could rely,
to look after the supplies and the sick brothers.

At the door he put other brothers,
whose speech was seasoned with salt,   Col 4.6
to receive visitors.
It was these porters who instructed those who came to be monks,
until Pachomius gave them the monk's habit.

In the same way, other faithful brothers
known for their love of God,
were named to carry out business and make purchases.

In each house the brothers who were serving
were changed every three weeks
and new ones appointed.

They carried out their tasks in obedience to the housemaster
and in the fear of God.
The others were appointed under the housemaster
to work in the shops and at the making of mats.
They were to be ready to undertake any obedience.
Pachomius himself gave three instructions a week,
one on Saturday and two on Sunday.
The housemaster gave instructions
on the two fast days, Wednesday and Friday, if they wished.

The nuns

27   Pachomius' sister, Mary, came north to see him at Tabennisi.
Pachomius sent the doorkeeper to say to her :
"You know that I am alive. You are not able to see me.
Do not be distressed.   If you want to share in this life,
the brothers will build you a cell, to live quietly there.
The Lord will no doubt call other women with you,
and because of you they will be saved.
There is no other hope in this world
but to do good before we depart from the body
and go to the place where we shall be judged,
and rewarded according to our works. "   Rom 2.6-7
When she heard these words, his sister wept.
Then she followed her brother's advice.
He built a monastery for her in the village
at a short distance from his own monastery.
It included a small oratory.
Gradually many other women came to live with her.
She remained their mother until her death.
Pachomius appointed an old man, Peter,
'his words seasoned with salt'   Col 4.8
to explain the Holy Scriptures frequently to them.
Pachomius wrote down for them the rules of the brothers
and sent them by the old man Peter for them to follow.

If a brother who was not yet one of the perfect
wanted to visit his relatives at the nuns' house,
Pachomius agreed with his housemaster and sent him to Peter.
They sat together until the visit ended, prayed, and went back.
No presents were given, for they owned nothing.
If there was some work to be done in the nuns' house,
Pachomius sent some capable and prudent brothers.
They went to do the work, and returned for their meal.

When a nun died,
the Mother covered the nun in a shroud.
Peter would send word to Pachomius,
who sent some old monks with him.
They grouped themselves at the entrance of the oratory.
The nuns were on the other side.
The brothers sang psalms
while the body was prepared for burial.
Then she was placed on a bier and carried to the mountain.
The men would lead the way, singing psalms.
The sisters followed behind the body, led by their Mother.
Then came Peter, who did not leave the sisters
until they had returned to their monastery.
The body was buried with prayers for the dead
and they returned, grieving.
After Peter's death,
Pachomius sent Titouë to look after the nuns.

Visit of the Archbishop

28   When St Athanasius was chosen Archbishop of Alexandria,
he sailed up the Nile as far as Aswan
in order to visit the churches.
He passed by Tabennisi, accompanied by a number of bishops.
Pachomius and his monks escorted him to the monastery,
singing psalms.

The Archbishop visited the church and all the cells.
Then Bishop Serapion kissed his hand and said:
"Holy Father, I ask you to make Pachomius a priest,
and to name him superior of this monastery in my diocese.
He is a man of God,
but in this one thing he will not obey me."
Pachomius hid himself in the crowd and disappeared.
Athanasius sat down and spoke to the crowd.
Then he stood up and prayed, and said to the monks :
"You will greet your Father and say this to him :
'So you hid from me, fleeing from any honour.
Then may the Lord grant you what you desire.
May you never have a rank.
When I return, if God wills,
I hope to have the joy of seeing you.'"
Then Athanasius left to go on south,
accompanied by the bishops
and a large crowd with lamps, candles and countless censers.
And Pachomius came out of his hiding-place.

Arrival of Theodore   G[1] 33,34

Theodore was born into an important christian family
in the diocese of Sne, and was greatly loved by his mother.
At the age of eight he was sent to school
so that he might learn to write. He learned well.
When he was twelve years old, on the day of the Epiphany,
there was a great family meal.
He was suddenly struck by a very strong feeling :
If you give yourself up to these dishes and wines
you will not see God's everlasting life.
He went away to a room apart and prayed :
'My Lord Jesus Christ, you alone know
that I want no part of this world.
It is you alone and your abundant mercy that I love.'

And he fasted like a monk every day until evening,
and sometimes ate only every other day.
When he was fourteen years old
he was allowed to leave home
and go to a monastery of hermit-monks in the diocese of Sne.
He was there for six years.

29 One evening the monks were sitting to speak the word of God
and afterwards Theodore heard one of them talking about
the holy man Pachomius he had seen at Tabennisi
and how Pachomius had explained the word of God.
Young Theodore when he returned to his cell
had a heart on fire with what he had heard that evening
about our father Pachomius,
his knowledge, his goodness,
how he would receive everyone
and show them the way to be pleasing to the Lord.
He prayed before the Lord in tears saying :
'Lord, if there is a truly holy man on earth,
allow me to live with him and be his servant.'

30 Some time later, Peter came south from Tabennisi
in the service of the brothers.
On his journey he went to ask hospitality
at the monastery where Theodore lived.
Theodore heard he was from Abba Pachomius' monastery.
At once he asked to go with him.
But Peter, learning that he was a son of an important family,
was afraid and said to him :
" I cannot take you with me on account of your parents."
Theodore held firmly to his idea in his heart
and when the party sailed north
he set out parallel to them along the river bank.
From the boat the brothers saw him and said to Abba Peter :
" There is the young man who asked to come north with you.
He has been keeping pace with us since morning."

At once Peter made them draw the boat to the shore,
and they took him on board.

32   When they arrived at Tabennisi
Abba Peter took him at once to our father Pachomius.
Theodore embraced him, kissed his hands and his feet,
and planted a kiss with great fervour
on the door of the monastery.
Seeing him in tears, Pachomius said to him :
" I will not stop you. Do not weep.
I am a servant of your father."
By this he meant God his Father.
Instructed by Pachomius who was an imitator of the saints
Theodore made great progress.   G^1 36
He was a wise young man who kept purity of heart,
he was measured and peaceable in his speech,
and obedient.
He became a comforter to many who were grieved, young and old.
Our father Pachomius realised in his heart
that God would put him in charge after himself.

37   After some time,
Theodore's mother obtained from the bishop of Sne
a letter addressed to our father Pachomius
to allow her son Theodore to come out and see her.
She had heard that among those monks
no one met his relatives again.
She came north with her other son Paphnouti.
When Pachomius had read the letter
he called Theodore and said :
" Doubtless you will go out
to meet your mother and your brother,
and all the more because the bishop has written about it."
Theodore feared breaking the Gospel commandment   Lk 14.26
so Pachomius did not urge it.

He gave orders for them to stay in his sister's monastery.
The mother saw her son
going out to work with the brothers.

38   Then Theodore's brother started running after him,
weeping and saying :
" I too want to become a monk."
Theodore treated him roughly,
but Pachomius said :
"Treat those come new to the monastery with care,
as one would treat a young tree."
Paphnouti was younger than Theodore and became a monk later.
Their mother wept for the loss of her sons,
since Paphnouti had left her as well
to become a monk along with Theodore.

Poverty

39   One day there was little bread : all had been given to the poor.
Pachomius said :
" The Lord will not leave us.
Meanwhile we will sell those two fine mats
that someone brought with him
when he came to join the brothers."
He passed all the night in prayer.
At early dawn while he was reflecting on the situation,
someone knocked on the monastery door and said :
" I was bringing some wheat for the workers in the mines,
but I saw in a dream that you need it.
Come, send down and take it from my boat.
I do not sell it to you. I give it to you,
with my greetings and those of my family.
You will pray for us."
Then they unloaded the boat
and Pachomius gave the man blessed gifts:
some cabbages and some other vegetables and a little bread.

Our father blessed him and he left quickly, full of joy.
Then our father Pachomius sat
and spoke the word of God to the brothers about the gift.
And the brothers marvelled at how quickly God had sent
the wheat they needed,
because of his holy servant Abba Pachomius.

Reception of visiting monks

40   Pachomius had a friend called Dionysius.
He was a holy priest of Nitentori,
a confessor of the faith, after the time of the martyrs.
He was saddened when he heard
that Pachomius no longer allowed monks from outside
to enter the monastery
but made them stay on their own by the monastery gatehouse.
He came to Tabennisi, and spoke to Pachomius about this.
Pachomius replied :
" It is the fruit of experience.
Do not think I want to grieve a man's soul, much less to grieve
the Lord who said :
Just as you did it to one of the least of these little brothers who
believe in me you did it to me.   Mt 25.40
But you know that there are many kinds of men
in the community:
old and young men, and the new monks.
They must not go through the monastery
talking to the new monks, who may shock them
because they do not yet understand what it is to be a monk.
That is why I said that it is good to let those who come to us
join us at prayer,
and then take them to a place apart for their meal.
After that they sleep in a place apart
and it is I who serve them,
as Abraham served the Lord under the tree

23

and not in his tent." Gen 18.1-8
Dionysius the priest was satisfied with the explanation,
recognising that Pachomius did everything **according to G**od.

Miracles of Pachomius

41   A woman of Nitentori had a continual flow of blood.
She asked the priest Dionysius to take her to Pachomius.
She was sure that if she saw him
the Lord would give her healing.
Dionysius agreed because he knew
the trouble she was suffering.
They got her into the boat and she came north with him.
After settling the matter of visiting monks
Dionysius and Pachomius sat talking outside the gatehouse.
The woman came up behind and touched his clothing
and because of her great faith she was cured.
Pachomius was very grieved
because he wanted no glory from men.

42   There was a small monastery near Tabennisi.
The superior often made visits to his friend Pachomius,
and the word of God he heard from his mouth
he would repeat to his own monks.
One day one of his monks told him he wanted to be steward
The superior did not consider him suitable for that task
but he was unable to persuade him.
So he tried to trick him. He said :
" Our Father Pachomius warned me not to give you this office.
He can see you are not worthy of the charge."
The monk grew angry and dragged him along saying :
" Come with me to Pachomius. He shall prove it to me."
The superior, worried, followed him to Tabennisi
along with another brother.
Pachomius was at work on part of the monastery wall.
The monk called up to him :

" Pachomius ! Come down to me
and tell me what I have done wrong !
Liar ! You say you see clearly
but you are stone-blind."   Jn 9.41
Pachomius understood nothing of all this.
At first he gave no word whatever in reply.
After a moment or two he said :
"Pardon me, my brother, if I have sinned against you.
Have you never sinned as well ?"
The angry brother calmed down.
Then Pachomius came down from the wall
and asked the superior privately :
" What happened to this brother ?"
The superior was embarrassed and explained to him :
"He wanted to be steward and he is unsuitable.
As he does not listen to what I say to him
I used your name."
Pachomius said to him then :
" Listen to me. Give him this office
to save his soul from the devil.
Charity supports and works for others.
Sometimes when we do good to a bad man
he comes to understand goodness.
Love of God is to have compassion for one another."   Eph 4.2
The superior accepted this.

A few days later the brother went back to Pachomius
to beg his pardon.
He kissed his hands and feet and said :
"You are a man of God, and greater than what we hear of you.
I am a sinner, and the Lord knows
if you had not been patient with me on the day I insulted you,
if you had spoken harshly to me,
I would have left the monastery and gone back to the world.

Blessed are you, man of God,
for thanks to your patience and goodness
the Lord has brought me to life."

45   Pachomius did many miracles and always with the prayer :
' Lord, if it is your will, heal the sick
for the glory of your name
and the progress of their soul.
Your will be done.'
But if this prayer was not granted by God, he did not feel sad.

46   Here is what he said often :
" The best healing is that of the soul.
— Idolatry is blindness :
it is unable to see the light of God.
If it learns by faith that God is truth
it recovers and is healed.
— The liar is dumb :
he is unable to speak the truth.
If he comes to speak the truth always, he is healed.
— The idle person is paralysed : unable to do any good work.
If he starts to practise the commandments he is healed.

Pachomius is sick

47   One day Pachomius went to cut reeds.
He returned ill and lay down.
Theodore wanted to cover him with a blanket. Pachomius said :
" Take that blanket off me and put a mat over me
like all the brothers,
until the Lord brings me relief."
Theodore did as he was told.
Then he wanted to give Pachomius some dates.
He refused with sadness and said :
" Because we have to take charge,

and serve the needs of the brothers,
do we have the right to give ourselves extras ?
Have you visited the brothers
and made sure that none of them is sick ?"
Pachomius remained sick in bed two days without food.
At intervals he would get up and pray, out of love for God.
On the third day he recovered, got up
and went out and ate with the rest.

48   Another time he was ill again
and in danger of death because of his great austerities.
They carried him to the infirmary.
He was surprised to find a brother there as thin as a skeleton,
he had been ill for so long.
The brother had asked for meat
but the infirmarian told him it was not permitted there.
Pachomius was surprised and grieved to hear this.
Just then they brought our father a few vegetables to eat.
He gave a sigh and said :
" You are respecters of persons.   Acts 10.34
Where is the fear of God ?
'You shall love your neighbour as yourself.'   Mt 19.19
Do you not see this brother is like a corpse ?
Why do you not give him what he asks ?
If you do not, I will not eat or drink either.
People who are sick need different things,
and 'to the pure all things are pure.'   Tit 1.15
If I had known what he wanted
I would not have left him in this sorry state."
When they heard this the brothers hurried to buy tender meat
and give it to the sick brother to eat.
And Pachomius ate his vegetables.

The foundation of Phbow and other monasteries

49   The number of brothers grew daily
at the monastery of Tabennisi.
Pachomius led some of them down river to the north
to the abandoned village of Phbow.
They built a large monastery there.
He named housemasters with assistants,
according to the rule of Tabennisi
He himself kept watch over the two communities.
The number of monks there grew very large.

50   A short time later, the aged superior
of the monastery of Sheneset, Abba Eboneh,
sent a message to Pachomius.
He asked him to accept his monastery into his congregation
and to give it his holy rule.
Pachomius took some brothers
and they stayed at Sheneset to teach observance of the rule.
He established the houses with housemasters
and their assistants,
according to the rule of the other two monasteries.
He directed them himself
often coming to visit and encourage them.

31   A great monk, Jonas,
superior of the monastery of Thmousons,
on the opposite bank of the Nile,
also sent for our father.
Pachomius went with three brothers.
He organised the monastery according to the rule in everything,
and often came to give help and spiritual aid.
52   Some time after this he built the monastery of Tse,
because of a vision from God,
according to the rules of the other monasteries.
He named as superior a great monk, very able, named Passo.

53   Arias, a bishop of the town of Shmin in the diocese of Sne,
      begged Pachomius to found a monastery there.
      He made a present to him of a small hut to come and visit him.
      While Pachomius was building the monastery with the brothers,
      carrying the clay on his back just as they did,
      some envious persons came to destroy during the night
      what had been done during the day.
      But through his patience
      Pachomius obtained protection from the Lord
      and the monastery was finished like the other monasteries.

56   There was in the diocese of Hew
      a holy man named Petronios.
      His parents were persons of rank and wealth,
      but he had built a monk's cell
      at the place called Thbew, on his parents' land,
      further north on the west bank of the Nile.
      He asked Pachomius to come
      so that he and his monks could join their congregation.
      His father, his brother, and their household, became monks.
      The father gave his cattle, his livestock, his material wealth
      and his boats.
      Pachomius organised everything,
      with housemasters and their assistants,
      according to the rule of the other monasteries.

57   Later, the Holy Spirit moved Pachomius
      to build a monastery at Tsmine near Theou, north of Shmin. *
      Petronios he sent from Thbew,
      and also made him superior of the two monasteries nearby.

---

* This was in fact the last of the monasteries of the pachomian congregation,
  nine in 383 (?345). Called the Great Monastery, it was at a distance from
  the others, in the region where Pachomius was born, also called Latopolis.

58   Some time later, leaving Apollonios in charge at Thbew,
     Pachomius began still another monastery, at Phnoum
     in the mountain desert of Sne, in the south.
     The bishop of the district
     had not asked him to build the monastery.
     He called a large crowd
     which came out to drive Pachomius from the place.
     Pachomius overcame the danger
     and built a very large monastery,
     with the rule of the other monasteries.
     He put at the head of the brothers
     an excellent monk named Sourous.

     In all, nine monasteries were founded.
     Pachomius went often to visit each of them
     like a nurse with her children,
     or 'as a mother gives warmth to her little ones'   1 Thess 2.7
     by loving with her whole heart.

Self-denial

59   One day Pachomius departed by boat with two brothers
     in order to visit Thmousons.
     At the hour for the evening meal
     the brothers ate some of everything before them,
     vegetables, cheese, figs, olives.
     Our father Pachomius ate only bread. And he began to weep.
     One brother looked up and saw him weeping.
     They asked : " Why are you weeping ?"
     He answered : " Because you are not dead to self,
     judging by the unrestrained way you ate.
     He who has his mind in heaven
     ought to practise a worthy abstinence   Col 3.2
     It is not a sin to eat, especially the cheap things,
     but it is good not to be dominated by anything,

as the Apostle says.
As for me, finding the bread good I was satisfied with it.
Another time I will eat according to the Lord's gift."

That night he said to the brothers :
" Shall we keep watch this evening ?"
They accepted.
Then he said to them :
" I know three ways of keeping watch,
from my days with the holy Abba Palamon.
You may choose one of them.
Either you pray from evening until midnight,
then sleep till the time of morning prayer.
Or you sleep until midnight and then pray until morning.
Or you pray a little and then sleep a little
and do this from evening until morning."
This last is what they chose
and the man of God arranged the times of sleeping and praying.
One of the brothers, overcome by sleepiness,
went off to sleep in the bottom of the boat.
The other persevered with our father until morning.
At the time of the morning prayer
they woke the one who had gone to sleep
and after the office the one who had watched all night
went to sleep in the bottom of the boat,
while the other rowed with our father
until they came to Thmousons, a long distance.

The superior, Cornelios, greeted Pachomius.
Then he asked the brothers, in a low voice :
" What has our father been doing ?"
The brothers answered :
" He has been a lesson to us."
Then they told their story,
and Cornelios exclaimed :

"What weakness afflicts men of these times ?
What ! Beaten by an old man at your age ?"
But that night Pachomius said to Cornelios :
" Do you want to keep watch with me tonight ?"
Cornelios agreed.
He set himself to pray.
The whole night passed
and still Pachomius continued his prayers.
Cornelios repeated all the texts he knew by heart.
Morning came and the signal was given for assembly.
Cornelios said to Pachomius :
" Father, what have I done ?
Why did you teach me such a lesson ?
I have not even had any water
since the evening meal yesterday."
Pachomius answered :
" Ah, Cornelios ! Beaten by an old man ?"
And Cornelios answered : " Pardon me, father .
I did wrong by not speaking to the brothers as I should."

60   When they left they went off to Phbow.
Pachomius appointed Paphnouti, Theodore's brother,
to assist him there in the administration of the monasteries,
for he was a very good and holy monk.

• THEODORE

61   Once Pachomius was lying sick.
So they brought him a plate of good meat and vegetables
seasoned with oil.
He said to Theodore :
" Bring me a jug of water."
He poured water on the plate so that the oil overflowed.
Then he gave the jug to Theodore saying :

" Pour water on my hands so that I may wash."
And as he was washing he threw water on Theodore's feet
as if to wash them clean.
Theodore said to him :
" What have you done, my father ?"
" I have put water on the food to remove the flavour
so that I will not be tempted by the desires of the flesh.
And when I washed my hands
I poured water on your feet to wash them
because it is I who must be the servant of all."   **Jn 13.12-16**

Theodore's wisdom and sympathy

Pachomius often corrected a brother of Phbow.
One day the brother said to Theodore :
" I cannot remain with that old man.
His words are too sharp."
Theodore said to help him :
" I also. He makes me suffer, and more than you.
We will go to find him and speak to him.
If he treats us with kindness, we will remain.
If he is too hard, we will depart together."
Theodore warned Pachomius.
That night they came to find him
and made some complaints to him.
Pachomius said to them :
" Yes, I was wrong. I ask your pardon.
But if you were good sons,
you would bear with your father."
And the brother was comforted.

63   One monk said to Pachomius :
" If you do not let me go home and see my family,
I will leave the monastery."

Pachomius said to Theodore :
" Accompany him to his parents' home
and do all that he wants, so as to bring him back to us.
He did not understand.
Be good to him, so that he does not go to the devil."
Theodore departed with the brother.
He accepted to eat in the same house as his parents
in order to please the brother.
On their return, Pachomius greeted Theodore
and told him he had done right.
Some days later,
Theodore discussed with the brother the Gospel words :
If anyone loves his father or mother more than me
he is not worthy of me.   Mt 10.37
The brother replied :
" This scripture has set the ideal high
so that we may manage part of it.
For how can we hate our parents ?"
Theodore went on :
" Is this truly the faith of our congregation ?
The Gospel says one thing and you do another.
If this is your faith
then I will go back to the little monastery from which I came.
The old men there never denied the Gospels."
The brother promised never again to go to his parents.

Problems of obedience

64   There was a monk who said many prayers
and performed much self-denial,
but through pride, in order to gain the respect of others.
Pachomius took him aside and said to him :
" The Lord said : I have come not to do my own will
but the will of him who sent me.   Jn 6.38
When God speaks to you through my mouth

34

he wants you to obey.

The devil is jealous. He wants to spoil all your efforts.

Now then, when you hear the sound for the midday meal
you will come to eat with the brothers.

Do not wait until evening.

Eat a little, though without taking your fill
in order to be master of your body, as you are vigorous.

Do that also at prayers : do what others do.

Do not remain at prayer after the office,
until you master the demon of boasting."

When it was time for the meal
the brother decided he would go with the others.

On the way he said to himself :

" I have not seen in Scripture :

' You shall not fast; you shall not pray.'"

So once again he followed his own judgment
and he did not go to eat with the brothers.

Pachomius was sad about the brother.

He called Theodore and sent him to him, saying :

" Go and see what the brother is doing.

If you find him at prayer, remain with him until I come."

Theodore found the brother at prayer.

He tried to speak to him.

The brother in anger cried out :

" Wicked one ! You stop me from my prayer ! "

He took up a big stone to throw at Theodore's head.

Theodore spoke severely to him in the name of the Lord.

At that moment in a cell nearby
a brother sang the beginning of the song of Moses :

' I will sing to the Lord ... '   Ex 15.1

Then the devil who was in the brother spoke himself :

" I am at work in those who sing for their own pleasure.

I am going to make this brother repeat that phrase nine times."

Indeed the monk repeated nine times : I will sing to the Lord .

Then Theodore wondered, awestruck :
' Who can escape the tricks of the devil ?'
At that moment Pachomius came.
He and Theodore prayed over the brother.   Jas 5
Then the Lord healed him and his eyes were opened.
He understood that he must act as a wise man
and no longer be a stupid one.
And he gave glory to God.

63   On another day, Pachomius went down into the monastery cistern
      in order to clean it, with the brothers.
      There was an old man who had lived long in the world
      and had been a monk only a short time.
      He began to complain :
      " That man is without mercy. He wants to kill us all."
      The following night the old man had a dream.
      He found himself standing over the cistern.
      He was looking down into it,
      and he saw a man, shining with light,
      in the midst of the brothers at their work.
      The man said to the brothers :
      " Receive the spirit of obedience and of strength."
      Then he said to the old monk : " And you,
      receive the spirit of faithlessness."
      Troubled by the dream,
      he came before the brothers at the evening prayer
      and confessed the whole thing.

Seeing into the future

66   Once our father Pachomius was busy with the brothers
      cutting reeds.
      At the end of their work they were returning to their boat
      while reciting the psalms,
      all loaded down with bundles of reeds,

following after Pachomius.
He put down his load of reeds and the brothers did the same,
standing and praying for a long time.
And Pachomius wept.
The brothers asked him : " Father, tell us what you saw."
He sat down and spoke to them.
" I saw the whole community in great pain.
Some were surrounded by great flames
they could not pass through.
Others were in the middle of them.
The points of thorns pierced them, leaving no way out.
And others, at the bottom of a great deep ravine,
were struggling desperately, unable to get out.
On the one hand the precipice was too steep
and on the other was a river
with crocodiles lying in wait for them.
Now my children, alas,
I think that after my death all this will happen to the Brothers."

Patience

67   A hermit came to visit Pachomius.
Pachomius welcomed him and said to Theodore :
" Go and prepare a meal for him."
But Theodore understood him to say :
Go and let me speak to him.
He went out and sat down. Pachomius called another brother.
The brother did not understand
any more than Theodore had done.
Then Pachomius prepared the meal himself.
He made the hermit eat and sent him away.
Then he called Theodore and said to him :
"Why did you disobey your father
when I told you to give the hermit something to eat ?"
Theodore said :

"Pardon me, my Father.
I understood you to say : Go,
so that I may talk with the hermit."
The other brother answered the same thing.
Pachomius said :
" The devil has willed to make me angry.
Thank God that he gave me patience.
That will teach you patience also."

He also said :
" I have heard that one devil said sadly to another one :
' I have a difficult man to deal with these days.
When I give him a bad thought
he goes to pray and weep before the Lord.
That makes me burn and I run away.'
The other devil said :
' When I give mine some advice
he listens to me always and does more still.
We are good friends.'
Therefore run from bad thoughts
and sign yourselves in the name of Christ.

Imagine a house with one hundred rooms.
If someone buys a room from the owner of the house
there is nothing to prevent him from entering it,
even though it is at the furthest end of the house.
In the same way, even if the faithful man
has all the fruits of the Holy Spirit,   Gal 5.22-23
if he lets the devil take only one fruit
perhaps he will take another,
because he has been weak with him.
But if on the other hand he pulls himself together again,
he will not only regain possession of his one fruit
which he has lost,
but will also make great progress."

68   The next day they again went to gather reeds
except one old man called Mauo, who was a housemaster.
He had lain down as if he was ill
but he was not ill, only indignant.
He said : " Why these long lectures ?
Are we in danger of falling every hour ?"
Then he saw a monk coming,
with another monk wearing a hair shirt.
The old man Mauo welcomed them.
' I can see that monk is very holy,' he said.
When Pachomius returned,
the stranger monk gave him a letter from his bishop.
The bishop wrote that the monk had committed a grave fault.
He was sending him to Pachomius for penance.
The monk confessed to Pachomius with tears.
Pachomius replied :
" We all fall very often.   Jas 3.2
But let us pray to the merciful God
and if we watch over ourselves in future,
he will hear us."
And he sent the monk away.
The old Mauo was astonished.
Our father Pachomius said to him :
" Because you are seated firmly on the rock,
do not think that everyone will find that way.
Let us pray the Lord full of mercy and pity
that he may save us from the snare of the evil one."
The old man replied :
" Forgive me for my ignorant behaviour."

Theodore's first instruction

69   One Sunday, Pachomius said to Theodore :
" When the brothers come out from table in the evening,
give your work to another brother and come to the assembly."

Theodore obeyed.
At the beginning of the assembly,
Pachomius took him by the arm and said :
" Stand here and speak to us the word of God."
Although unwilling,
Theodore spoke according to the inspiration of the Lord.
All listened to him standing, and Pachomius also.
But some proud brothers were dissatisfied
because Theodore was so young.
They did not want to listen and returned to their cells.
This was when Theodore was thirty-three years old.
But Pachomius knew he was more advanced in holiness.
After the assembly, Pachomius said :
" You are foolish not to listen.
The words that were said in the instruction,
are they words from a young man
or the words of Theodore ?
Was it not said :
' Whoever receives a child in my name receives me ?'
I listened with all my heart
like someone thirsty for cold water."

70   After that, Pachomius named Theodore steward of Tabennisi
      and his words were full of grace.
      Pachomius stayed at Phbow, the principal monastery,
      in order to direct the congregation of nine monasteries.
71   He took Paphnouti with him
      in order to sell the products of work from all the monasteries
      and to buy food for them.
      All the brothers came to Phbow twice yearly :
      at Easter to celebrate the feast in common,
      and 13 August at the end of the harvest
      to give their accounts in detail
      and receive their instructions for work.

Pachomius often visited the monasteries
in order to encourage the brothers and regulate problems.

An act of humility

72   One day, Pachomius came to Tabennisi
and sat down to weave mats as he usually did.
A young brother came to tell him :
" My Father, we no longer weave like that any more.
Our Father Theodore told us to do it this way."
Pachomius immediately stood up and said :
" Very well. Come and sit down and show me."
The young brother showed him.
Pachomius did not scold the young monk
for speaking out of turn
but set to work and did as he was told.

Brother Elias

The same day, after work,
he explained to the brothers the Holy Scriptures.
Then he said to them :
" Concerning the cause for which I came here today :
what I sought is in an earthenware jar."
Now Brother Elias, who was simple-minded,
had taken five figs and put them in a jar and hidden it.
When he heard Pachomius' words
he went out to find the jar with the figs
and said in front of all the brothers :
" Forgive me, my Father,
the Lord knows this is all I have taken.
Now I have made known my fault to you."
Pachomius and the brothers were surprised and Pachomius said
" I tell you for certain that I knew nothing about it
but the Lord gave me the means to correct this brother
so that he is no longer mastered by food.

73   For a long time, every day after work,
      Theodore came to Phbow.
      Pachomius gave him the word of God
      and he repeated it to the brothers of Tabennisi in the evening.   *

A martyr who ran away   G¹ 85

Once, the barbarians were making war.
They found a monk from another place and took him prisoner.
Then they started to drink wine, and said to him :
" Come, offer some wine to the gods
and pour yourself a drink."
He refused. They wanted to cut his throat.
The monk was afraid.
He offered drink to the gods of the barbarians.

When the men were drunk, he escaped.
His heart was sad. He was unable to pray,
because it is written :
' He who disowns me, I will disown him.'   Mt 10. 32,33
Desperate, he came to the monastery
and told Pachomius all the story.
Pachomius said to him :
" Unhappy man. The crown was brought to you
and you did not take it.
Why did you not die courageously for him who died for us ?
You have suffered a great loss.
Do not despair of yourself,
but now, do penance, for the Lord desires not our death
but our repentance."

---

* The distance between the two monasteries was only two miles.
   Theodore had been nine years at Tabennisi.

42

Theodore asked Pachomius one day about a headache he had.
Pachomius replied :
" Do you think that a pain or anything like that
comes without God's permission ?
Bear it therefore.
When he wills, he will heal you.
And if he tests you for a while
thank him like that perfect man Job
who bore everything that came upon him
and blessed the Lord.   Job 1.21
Indeed although the one who bears the cross
may not be suffering for anything in particular,
the cross and the exercise in self-control suffice for him.
But one who lies sick can be struggling far more
than one in good health,
in courage and in patience.
Then such a one has a double crown.
It is good for the one who suffers to bear pain about ten years
before speaking of it."   *
And Theodore was comforted by these words.

The importance of silence

74   It happened once in the bakery of Tabennisi
when Theodore was in charge
that some brothers working there
talked at the time when they should be reciting prayers.
Pachomius was at Phbow,
but he knew what they were doing.
When Theodore went to see him, he said to him :

---

* An example of the extreme sayings of the Desert Fathers to make a point
  when teaching others. They gave the sick the remedies they could.

" You have not kept the rule.
This evening, go and see the Brothers
who are talking in the bakery."
Theodore found in fact that five brothers were talking.
Pachomius said to him :
" Do those brothers think that these are human matters ?
When you obey you do the will of God.
Even if an order is about a very small thing
it is important.
In order to obey Joshua
the army kept silence for seven days,
going around Jericho.   Josh 6.1-21
Then when they received the order to shout
they obeyed and fulfilled God's will."

77   It happened again another time, in the bakery of Tabennisi :
eighteen brothers failed in silence.
An angel warned Pachomius.
He took Theodore from the charge of the bakery
and sent him to his cell.
There he fasted and prayed for two days together
for the fault of his brothers.
This he did for three weeks. Then Pachomius said to him :
" It is enough. But be more watchful
or you will be guilty of sin before the Lord Jesus Christ."

Theodore second to Pachomius at Phbow

78   When Pachomius saw that Theodore had made great progress
he put Sourous the Younger in his place at Tabennisi
and took Theodore with him as his assistant at Phbow
in order to help him as Joshua helped Moses.   Josh 1.1
He sent him often to the other monasteries,
to encourage the brothers by the word of God.
It was he who accepted or sent away the postulants,

44

under the inspiration of God and of Pachomius.
Pachomius once said :
" Theodore and I, we will fulfil the same service
to the honour of God."
He had the authority to give orders as father of the monasteries.

The brothers were happy G^1 91
when Theodore came to the monasteries,
because he had received from God the gift of great kindness.
Pachomius was perfect in all things
but he was sad in his manner and severe,
because he thought always of those who fall into hell
for their sins.

Moderation

79   One day, Theodore saw a young strong novice
eating many leeks at table.
He said to the brother :
" A monk must not eat many leeks
because that makes the body strong and the soul weak."
He said this leaning against the wall
because it was a hot day
and he was fasting for two days together.
While he was speaking, Pachomius arrived.
When he saw Theodore he said sadly :
" Is it the wall that will support your body ?"
Theodore straightened up immediately.
He was very sad over the brother he had blamed
for eating too many leeks.
Perhaps it was not God's will he should speak so,
he said to himself.
'Why did I not wait for the Lord to move him to choose freely
and follow the good ways of the other brothers ?'

80   One day, Theodore saw a brother go past
with his cloak over his shoulder.
He asked him : " Where are you coming from ?"
Pachomius had heard.
After the brother had gone on,
he called Theodore and said to him :
" Theodore, make haste to be master of your heart
with all moderation.
It is not good to ask unnecessary questions.
Speak only for the salvation of souls, because it is written :
One who is faithful in small things
will be faithful in great. "

Lk 16.10

The death of a catechumen

81   A catechumen brother was dying.
It was the custom to bring all the catechumens of the monasteries
to Phbow to baptise them during the Forty Days.
Pachomius and Theodore came to see him at Thmousons.
The superior of the monastery said to Pachomius :
" We are afraid to take him to Phbow for the baptism :
he will die on the way. "
Pachomius said : " Why not baptise him here ?"
The superior said : " There is no priest here."
Then Pachomius and Theodore saw angels
who had come to fetch him
and to baptise him before he left his body.
Pachomius understood that the brother catechumen
had entered into the rest of the saints.
His body was carried to the mountain
and he was buried with the other brothers.

83   Another day, Theodore heard a beautiful song in the air.
He went at once to Pachomius.
Pachomius said :
" It is a righteous soul that has left its body

and the angels are passing with it above us.
We have had the grace to hear those
who are blessing God in front of it. "
They looked up
and recognised the one who had passed.

The guardian angel of the monastery

84   One night Theodore rose and made a tour of the brothers.
He prayed standing, keeping watch by them.
In his prayer he had a vision :
All the brothers were lying down like resting sheep,
and an angel was watching over them.
And the angel said : " Is it you
who are watching over the brothers
or is it I ?"
Theodore returned then into his cell, saying :
'Truly we only appear to be watching.
In reality it is the angels who are our shepherds
and watch over us, the sheep of God's flock.
It is they who keep us safe
from the wicked snares of the enemy.'

85   Again, another day, Pachomius sent Theodore
to a monastery of Sne, Thashmin,
to visit the brothers about an important matter.
While he was praying near a fig tree in this monastery
he looked into the distance
and saw our father Pachomius at Phbow, some sixty miles away.
He was sitting and speaking the word of God to the brothers,
and Theodore also heard the words he was saying to them.
When he returned south
he repeated all the words he had heard him say.
Pachomius replied :
" Yes, it is exactly what I said."

Gluttony

87   One day after work, Theodore made porridge
for those brothers who could not eat bread.
A young strong brother named Patloli,
constantly at war with the passions of youth,
had the desire to eat a bit of the porridge.
The Spirit of God in his conscience warned him :
" That has been made for those who need it,
but you have no need of it."
But he did not obey the thought prompted in him by the Lord.
Instead he went and ate some with the brothers.
When the brothers had finished eating
they went as usual to hear the words of God from Theodore,
and ask him to tell them their faults.
To some he would say :
" You are faint-hearted."
To others : " You are quick to get angry."
Or : " You are harsh in speech."
And then he said :
" I see one among you who puts all his hope in a cooking-pot."
At once the brother understood this was meant for him.
He quickly knelt down among them all, saying :
" Pray for me, for I took no notice of my conscience.
Because I disobeyed the good suggestion that came from my heart
the Lord has rebuked me in public."

Vision of hell

88   Still another day, by the Lord's command,
our father Pachomius was carried away
that he might contemplate the punishments and tortures
which the children of men may have to undergo.
Having been brought to the north of paradise
far from the world and the firmament,
he saw rivers canals and ditches filled with fire.

In them the souls of sinners were being tormented
If some of the souls which the torturing angels were tormenting
lifted their heads above the fire
they would whip them hard
and thrust them further into the fire.

He likewise saw monks undergoing punishment in that place
and he questioned the angel who was walking with him.
The angel answered :
" Those whom you see are quite pure as regards the body,
but they are idlers and go about in places where brothers are
and speak ill of other brothers,
with the hope of getting food and drink."

The torturing angels are quite filled with joy and gladness.
When souls are brought in and turned over to them
they are overjoyed, happy over their downfall.
When he had gone on a little
Pachomius saw an innumerable crowd of souls of all ages
being roughly hurried along by the pitiless torturing angels.
And he was told :
" These are the souls of sinners who died today
throughout the world
and they are being classified for punishment
according to what they deserve.
They utter loud cries:
'Woe to me for not knowing the God who created me
that I might be saved. '"

When the angel had finished showing Pachomius all the punishments
he counselled him urgently, saying :
" Pachomius, bear witness to the brothers
and to the whole world,
so that they may do penance and be saved."

From that day on
when Pachomius assembled the brothers for instruction
he spoke first on the Scriptures
and then he would tell them about the sufferings he had seen
so that they might have the fear of God and avoid sinning.

• THEODORE THE ALEXANDRIAN

89   There was another Theodore,
a young man who had been born a pagan but became a Christian
and who was Reader for twelve years in the church of Alexandria,
under Archbishop Athanasius.
He heard about the congregation Pachomius had founded
and longed to live with these monks.
Some time later Pachomius sent some brothers to Alexandria
with a little boat
to visit the Archbishop and buy a few things
for the needs of the sick brothers.
Theodore went up to them and, through an interpreter,
because he spoke greek and not coptic,
he asked to go with them to join Pachomius.
The Archbishop gave him leave
and sent a letter about him to Pachomius.
There was one old monk who spoke greek
and he taught him coptic and all the rules of the brothers.

Theodore the Alexandrian told Pachomius :
" The monks of Alexandria are quite firm
in the orthodox faith of the holy Catholic Church of Christ.
As regards their food,
there are plenty of good things on their table.
They eat and drink well
in accordance with what is written :
These things God has provided for his faithful

that they might partake of them with thanksgiving." 1 Tim 4.1
Then our father Pachomius said :
" Is it possible for them to eat and drink without measure
and still keep their purity ?"
He struck the ground with a stick he had in his hand saying :
" If this ground is watered and manured
it will become fertile and produce plants.
It is the same with the body.
If it is gladdened with abundance of dishes, drinks and rest,
it will not be possible for us to keep it in purity."
Theodore was amazed.

Some time later,
some of the brothers went off to Alexandria as usual.
When they returned
Theodore asked about some of the brothers there :
" How are they doing at present ?"
They said that some of them had been caught in impure actions
and people told bad tales about others of them.
And Theodore admired Pachomius' wisdom
and how he said it is impossible
for those who eat and drink well
to practise perfect purity.

Abba Pachomius made every effort to learn greek,
and encouraged Theodore frequently.
When he noticed that he had made good progress
in divine knowledge
he appointed him superior of the house of the Alexandrians
and the foreigners who came after him, Romans and Armenians.
This was thirteen years before Pachomius died.

90 Pachomius taught this Theodore the way to form the brothers
    who were placed under his authority.

One day he told him privately :
" It is a great matter if you see one of your house is careless
and do not take care to instruct him.
If he gets angry, be patient with him,
waiting for him to be touched by the Lord.
It is just as when someone wants to draw a thorn
from somebody's foot.
If he draws out the thorn and it causes bleeding
the person has relief.
If he does not succeed in removing it
he applies ointment and, with patience,
the thorn comes out gently by itself.
But if the offence is serious, report it to me,
and we will do as God inspires me.

> Take greater care of the sick than of yourself.
> Be pure at all times.
> Bear the cross more than they do since you hold the rank of a father.
> Be the model for all that the brothers do.

And if there is anything you want to decide
and you do not know how,
inform me, and with God's grace,
we will go at it together
until we find the answer and put it in practice."

91   One day Theodore said to Pachomius :
" It appears that Cornelios prays during the whole of the office
without any distractions.
I have tried very often,
but after three psalms I am always distracted."
Pachomius said to him :
" When a poor person sees a prince he envies the prince.
When a prince sees a king he envies the king.
It is a long time that Cornelios has had to struggle.
You can be like him by imitating him.

And always be grateful to God
and keep his commandments with all your heart.
With time, you will become like Cornelios."

92   There were at Phbow two ancient brothers
who had a great way of life and were pure in heart,
but they often used to grumble at our father Pachomius
because of his corrections.
The man of God Pachomius took upon himself
night watches, prayers and fasting before the Lord
for their healing.
One after another, they all died in the peace of God.

Once at Tabennisi   G[1] 96
our father spoke about various thoughts :
desire for power, kindness, hatred of another, love of money.
He said :
" Just as fire cleanses off all rust
and makes the object shine,
so the fire of God consumes every evil in us
and makes us into a vessel for special occasions
and ready for every good use.   2 Tim 2.21; Phil 4.18
If a man does not consult a man of experience
on how to overcome the temptings of the enemy
and is not vigilant,
even though he may love God,
it will ruin him.
Let him say to the demons :
'These thoughts are not mine but yours.
You will be punished in eternal fire.
But I shall not cease blessing, praising and thanking God
who created me.'
When we say such things with faith
the demon vanishes like smoke."

93   One day, Pachomius came to a monastery
for the burial of one of the brothers.
He did not allow the brothers to sing psalms for him
to bless him.
He collected the monk's clothes in the middle of the monastery
and burned them,
putting fear into the brothers lest they neglect their life.
Then he said :
" That brother led a bad life.
I had warned him often but he had not listened.
He gave in to the heat of his passions.
He was a worldly monk."
And the careless brothers were filled with great fear.

• THEODORE OF SNE DOES PENANCE

94   It was seven years since Theodore of Sne
was appointed associate to Pachomius at Phbow.
Then the Lord sent him a great test.

One day Pachomius was ill,
so ill that he was in danger of death.
Then all the superiors of the monasteries
and the brothers who were at Phbow
gathered about Theodore and said to him :
" If the Lord visits our father,
promise that you will take our father's place.
Then we shall not be a flock without a shepherd."
For a long time Theodore gave them no reply at all.
But after much asking, he ended by consenting.
When Pachomius got a little better from his illness
he heard about this.
He said to the brothers :

" Let each of you tell his faults, and I will begin.
I am often negligent in visiting the brothers."
In turn, Theodore replied :
" For seven years now I have been sent by you
to visit the monasteries and to settle everything as you do.
But now I am plagued with the thought :
'After him, I will be in charge '
and I have not been able to conquer it yet."
Abba Pachomius told him :
" Very well. You no longer have authority over anything.
Go away by yourself somewhere
and pray to the Lord that he may forgive you."

Theodore went off to a solitary place
where he fasted often and wept.
Seeing him shed so many tears,
one brother said to himself :
' It must not happen that he cuts himself off from the brothers,
and goes away as a result of this sorrow.'
When during the night Theodore would come out for some need
the brother followed him to watch him in case he went away.
He spent two years in that punishment
and the seniors encouraged him often.
The punishment was to make him perfect
and completely free of ambition for power.

Abba Titouë came also and encouraged him saying :
" Do not be sad, Theodore, over what our father has done to you.
The Lord knows that if you persevere in humility,
thanking the Lord for what has happened to you,
you also will be blessed like Job, the just man. "   Job 42.16-17
95   While Theodore was still doing penance
Pachomius, to comfort him, sent him to Thmousons
to visit the brothers and see how they were doing.

55

When he reached Sheneset he sat down on the river bank
to wait for the ferry boat to take him over.
There were two old men in the boat.
One said to his companion :
" The story goes concerning a farmer
that he was very harsh in all things.
Every man who came to work under his orders for a year
would go away after a while and work with him no more.
Then there was someone who made a courageous resolution saying :
'I will go with him and put in a full year.
I will go along with him in everything he commands me to do
until I get to know how he works.'
Then he worked with him with all patience.
After submitting him to various trials
and seeing that he was not faint-hearted
and did not turn back,
but on the contrary put up with him till the year's end,
the farmer said to him :
'Now I understand that you are capable of staying with me always
because you acted in all things according to my wishes.
The two of us have become like one.
You will be my son and have my property.'
And the man remained working with him all the time.

The explanation of the parable is this :
The farmer is God.
He sends trials and hard things
to those who want to serve him well.
He puts them to the test so that they may be able to endure him
when he opposes their will in everything,
so that they always do his will.
So then, if this monk here bears everything his father tells him
he too will become chosen and blessed
before his Lord Jesus Christ."

While the two old men were talking
Theodore remained seated far from them
listening, head on knees,
and he was comforted by what they said.
When the ferryboat reached the landing-place
Theodore stepped off the boat, and saw them no more.
He went on his way until he reached Thmousons
weeping because of the sweetness of the words he had heard.
He visited the brothers according to our father's command,
then returned to Phbow, greatly comforted.

96 One day, when the small boat was about to set off for Alexandria,
Zachaeus, the head of the boatmen monks,
came to Pachomius and said :
" The eyes of Theodore have been harmed with weeping.
If you permit me I will take him away with us to Alexandria.
He will work with the boatmen."
On the boat, Theodore's attitude to the others was very humble.
When they sat down to table to eat
they would yield place to him
to serve himself first
but he would refuse to serve himself until all had done so.
Many times he would spend the night reciting the Scriptures.
Every time they had to moor the boat in the course of the trip
it was he who jumped out onto the bank first
to tie the boat to the stake.
When he came to Alexandria the Archbishop saw him
because he had often heard of him.
He wrote a letter to our father Pachomius
in which he praised Theodore.

On their return from Alexandria
Pachomius asked Zachaeus and Theodore :
" How is the Church there ? "
For he was anxious for the Church at that time.

He prayed to God for the Church
because the Arians had risen up like bandits against it.
They replied :
" Some Arian heretics with a certain Gregory
have attacked the Church violently like robbers.
They have taken its Christ-bearer, Archbishop Athanasius."
Pachomius' heart was deeply sad
that the people of God were being so wronged.
He prayed to God for the peace of his catholic church.
He would say :
" We believe in the Lord.
He has permitted this to happen in order to test the believers.
The punishment of the heretics will come soon."
Before long indeed
the Archbishop returned to his church with honour. *

97   After that, Pachomius said to the brothers :
" Theodore is humble in the eyes of men
but he has not lowered his eyes from the Lord.
On the contrary, he has made progress seven times over."

•   **LAST YEARS**

Prayer for the world

100   A day came when a great food shortage, spreading disease
was on them.
All the while that the famine lasted outside

---

* This trip to Alexandria was made during the year 346. Gregory had taken
possession of Athanasius' archiepiscopal see in March 345. Athanasius
returned the next year from exile.

Pachomius mourned and fasted with abundant prayer,
fulfilling the words of the Apostle : If one member suffers
all the members will suffer with it.   1 Cor 12.26
He also prayed the Lord with great insistence
that the level of the waters of the Nile
might rise to a good height
so that there would be abundance of crops.

101   Every time he prayed, our father Pachomius
would remember the words of St Paul :
Pray for everyone.   1 Tim 2.1
He used to pray for the whole world, grouping his intentions :
In the first place for monks and nuns.

He asked the grace of the Lord
to keep them firm to the promise which they had made in their heart.

For married people
he asked faithfulness to the law of the Gospel.

He prayed for all those who have begun well,
so that the cares of the world would not prevent them
from achieving their goal of doing good and reaching heaven.

He prayed for all those who do the work of the devil,
for non-christians, and for heretics who did not understand
and were led astray,
so that they would be made worthy through the fruit of penance
and remember the good that God shows them in nature
and in helping them with their work.

He prayed for kings and the leaders of the world,
so that they would resemble those just kings
David, Hezekiah and Josiah
and those like them who practised righteousness.

He prayed for the clergy of the catholic church
that God would 'open a door to his word'.   Col 4.3

So he prayed for the whole world.

102   There were ten of the brothers at Phbow
who were careless and thought wickedly
and had no faith in Pachomius' teaching.
He prayed for them.
One of the old monks of Phbow came to him to say :
" These ten brothers live in carelessness.
Why do you not drive them out ?"
But he answered :" The saints are models for us.
You know well what Moses ended by doing
when his people had sinned :
he gave up his soul in order to save them."   Ex 32.32
He continued to pray for those brothers
in order that they would repent and be saved.

Peace of God and peace from the devil

After some time,
Pachomius happened to meet one of the ten careless brothers
and said to him pleasantly :
" How are you doing, my son ?"
The brother replied :
" My heart is at peace
thanks be to God and to your holy prayers."
But Pachomius said to him :
" In the past you resisted the devil.
Then he made war every day on you.
Now, you have opened the door to him,
so he is installed in you.
That is why you feel at peace."
The brother begged to know what penance he should do
and Pachomius told him to fast two days together.
This he did for a while,
though he still doubted the word of the man of God
till the day of his death.

Vision of heresies

103   One day, Pachomius saw a vision of a great black hole,
with a pillar in the middle.
And there were in the place many men
unable to see where to go to find the light.
And voices sounded from all sides saying :
' Here is the door, here, close to us !'
They would all turn back to find it, and hear the voice again,
and turn back another time.
Some who were in the darkness went round and round the pillar
thinking they were going to the light.
Then he saw his whole community following a lamp.
Four of them could see it and the others followed them,
each holding onto his neighbour's shoulder
because they were in the darkness.
If one let go, all those behind him went astray.
And Pachomius called out to them to hold on
and not lose themselves and the others behind.
Guided by the lamp in this way
they came to an opening and the great light above.

He told these things to some of the brothers in private
and we heard it from them much later,
with the following interpretation :
This world is the dark place.
Because of error, each heretic thinks to have the right path.
The lamp is faith in Christ
which saves and leads to the kingdom of God.

The regular life

104   Pachomius instructed the brothers every day
in the science of the saints.
He worked on their spirit as a good farmer cares for his field
and drives off robbers and birds.

He gave the brothers laws and customs
which they learned by heart as they did the Gospels.

He also recommended that anyone who broke them
should be punished
according to the seriousness of the fault,
in order to obtain for him pardon from the Lord.

Those who made journeys outside
did not give the brothers news of the outside world.

When a brother received a letter or a present from his parents
the Superior had to be told about it first.
He saw if it was good for the brother
or, if it was not, nothing was said to him.

The brothers lived according to the Rule
without disagreement, without worldly worries,
and already as if in heaven.

Useless words

105   One day, a brother said to some of the others :
" It is the season for grapes."
Pachomius said :
" Why do you trouble your brothers ?
You make them envious, so they want to eat the fruit.
It is a word which can do no good to anyone.
One day the Lord will say to you :
'You have injured your soul and that of your brother
with your joking.'
I tell you, every little word of this kind, or any unkind remark,
ruins the soul before God.
You are like an invited guest
who has damaged some container.
His host will say to him :
' What ! I have invited you to eat and drink

and you have damaged the dish. How ungrateful !'
Those I have brought together for their salvation,
are you going to ruin them
by your ruinous words ?"

Pachomius said to the brothers :
" The glory and the merits of good cenobites
are greater than those of hermits.
But if they do not act rightly,
they give greater scandal than those who follow the hermit life.
When a merchant sells on the market from day to day
bread, vegetables and other things,
he does not become very rich
but he will earn a living.
So it is with a hermit.
He does not have charge of others,
but neither is he trained by their example.
The purity of his life, his fasting, his prayers, his self-denial
will receive their reward in the eternal life,
but he does not earn therefore a higher place
in the kingdom of heaven.
That, then, is a parable on the little brother cenobites.
They do not practise great and excessive self-denial
but walk in obedience, love and purity
according to the established Rule.
They are the favourite servants of the king.
They are kept in the king's palace and go freely there
while the great rulers do not enter
without telling the servants.
The hermits believe that these brothers are less perfect
and that their way is lower than that of the hermit.
In reality the cenobites are found perfect in the law of Christ
because of their faithfulness
and their continual submission to God.

They are far superior to the hermits
because they are always serving one another
as it is written : Serve each other in sweetness and patience
before the Lord Jesus Christ.   Eph 4.2,32

But I am going to show you also the faults of the cenobites
who make scandal greater than the hermits do in their cells.
When a merchant journeys in all weathers,
if his boat has not had any accident
he becomes very rich.
But if he is shipwrecked all his riches disappear with him.
So the cenobite who makes great progress,
and puts no stumbling-block nor scandalises anyone,
gains imperishable riches.
If he scandalises only one brother,
unhappiness will come to him for his carelessness."

107   A brother said to Pachomius :
    " You have dismissed a hundred brothers this year.
    Before long we shall have no one in the community."
    Pachomius replied :
    " The opposite is true. If I had let them stay
    the brothers would have diminished in numbers.
    When the bad ones are numerous
    they draw the anger of God on the good.
    If I did not dismiss the bad ones
    even the good ones would become like them."
    But the brother continued :
    " But why do you dismiss the weaker postulants ?"
    Pachomius answered :
    "It is not that I refuse what I call the darnel   Mt 13.27
    but because their passions rule them.
    They are no good in the cenobitic life.
    Even if someone is a bad offspring of his parents

it is possible for him to change by his own will and judgment,
whatever his nature may be.
If I leave the good in order to occupy myself with the bad,
the good will fall into sin.
The farmer does not abandon his good field
in order to clear a field full of sand and thorns.
Sometimes, however, I am able to accept one or two weak ones.
I have to struggle long in order to save them.
I go to see them often, day and night.
If I have to send them away
I always say :
' You have not come to be a monk with all your heart
You must do penance
but not in the house of the cenobites.
Leave and be a hermit somewhere.
Fast and pray with tears ay and night for a long time.
God will pardon you, but not here.'"

Usefulness of illnesses

111   One day, Pachomius prayed for the healing of a man who was ill.
During his prayer, an angel said to him : " Do not ask that.
The Lord has sent him this illness for his salvation.
If he is cured, he will regret it greatly."
Then Pachomius said to the sick monk :
" The Lord has sent you this illness for your soul's salvation.
Do not be grieved.
Thank the Lord and say to him :
'Blessed be the Lord of my salvation.'"   Ps 17 **46**

A persecution   G¹ 112

113   As Pachomius' fame spread far and people talked about him
some would say exaggerated things.
There arose a debate about his visions

65

and being able to see into men's souls.
He was summoned to answer this in the church of Latopolis
in the presence of monks and bishops. *
He answered humbly and with confidence.
When he stopped speaking, a man possessed
came at him with a sword.
But the brothers saved him.
An uproar started in the church.
Some said one thing, some another...
The brothers made their escape
and went to their last monastery, the one called Phnoum
which is in the district of Latopolis.

Vision of Heaven

114   One day, Pachomius fell ill.
The angels sent to fetch him, carried away his soul.
He died, and he was taken into another world
above and beyond this one.
He saw the cities of the saints
and fine buildings it was not possible to describe,
and all the good things
for those who love God.   1 Cor 2.9
He remembered the parable where it says :
Enter into the joy of your master.   Mt 25.21,23
That world is so large it is without limits.
Our world is as nothing in comparison.
The climate is temperate and the air sweet.
The fruit trees and the vines never die

---

*   The Synod of Latopolis took place in the year 345, less than a year before
   Pachomius' death.
   Phnoum was the last of the nine foundations made by Pachomius. It was
   also the one farthest up the Nile.

and produce food for the spirit
with much more beauty and variety than the trees of this world.
They are never without fruit and give out great fragrance,
a perfume unbearably sweet
if the Lord did not give the strength for it.
There is no day nor night in that world.
The light is not from sun or moon
but radiant and continual.
The Lord lightens that world as Isaiah says :
The Lord will be our everlasting light.   Is 60.19-20

As Pachomius approached the gate of life,
God gave an order for him to return to his body.
Pachomius became sad
because he had no desire to return to his body
because of the unbearable beauty and splendour
of the city and the light.
A man who was in charge of the door
turned to look at him.
The face of that man shone with great splendour
and his body was all light.
He said to him :
" My son, return to your body.
It still remains for you to undergo
a small martyrdom in the world."
Pachomius was glad
because he had a great wish to be a martyr for the Lord's name.
The angels rejoiced with him. And they told him :
" That is the Apostle Paul."
As soon as they brought it to the place where his body was,
the soul considered its body, and it was dead.
The soul drew near the body.
All the members opened up
and the soul again took its place in the body,

and Pachomius was alive.
While Pachomius' soul had been carried away
the brother who was with him slept.

Final sickness and death of Pachomius

117   By God's permission a sickness struck the monasteries.
It was the plague.
Each day there were two to four deaths in the monastery.
Sourous, the father of the monastery of Phnoum, died.
Cornelios, superior of Thmousons,
and Paphnouti the steward of all the monasteries,
and many other great monks, died.
When the fever took them, they changed colour,
their eyes became bloodshot,
they choked and died like someone being strangled.
About 130 died in the epidemic at Phbow.

Pachomius also fell ill.
As usual, he did not believe that he was ill.
He said nothing, and because of his strong will
he went to harvest with the brothers.
During the work he fell on his face.
The brethren were afraid.
They ran to him and lifted him from the ground.
They found he had a high fever.
They brought him to the monastery.
He did not want to be laid on a bed, like the other sick monks.
So they placed him on the ground.
One of them sat fanning him with his hood.

118   The illness lasted many days.
It was during the Forty Days of Lent.
He spent the last four days of the Passover without eating,
praying for the unity of the community.

The brothers of all the monasteries had come
to celebrate Easter at Phbow.
On Friday evening they all gathered round him,
and he gave them his last counsels.
He said to them :
" My brothers and my sons,
I believe that the time has come
for me to go the way of all the earth
like all my fathers.   1 Kgs 2.2
You will know that I have always walked among you
in humility and self-denial.
You know that I have never sought an easier life than any of you.
We all live as one man.
I do not say this through pride.
God is my witness.
I have never given anyone bad example,
neither before God nor before man.
All the observances that I have prescribed for salvation
were for the good of your souls.
You know that I have never corrected any of you
as the one having authority, except for the good of his soul.
Neither have I changed any of you
from one monastery, cell or employment to another,
except for your good before God.
I have not returned evil for evil.
When I was insulted, I said :
He does not sin against me but against God.
And I have not been angry,
I accepted reproaches as coming from God.
When journeying, I never asked for a donkey,
as one having authority,
but I walked gratefully and humbly.
When one of you caught up with me and brought me a donkey
I did not accept

if I was not ill or truly hard pressed.
For food, drink, dress and ease,
you know well how it was with me."
While he was saying these things, Theodore was seated near him.
He kept his head on his knees,
and he wept.
Many of the other brothers wept also.
They recalled with what love
Pachomius had always come to serve each one,
and his great humility
when he acted as the servant of each of them
in the fear of the Lord, as Paul says :
We have become as children among you.
As a mother cares for her children we have tried to give you
not only the Gospel of God but our own soul as well,
because of our love for you.   1 Thess 2.7,8

120   Theodore waited on Pachomius during his last illness.
He was lying in the infirmary where all the sick brothers were.
He asked Theodore to treat him the same as the other brothers.
He received the same care as they did in everything.
There were no differences at all made between them
as he had earlier given instructions.
At the end of about forty days, his body was very weak
but his heart and his eyes were like a burning light.
One day he asked Theodore for another cover
because the one he had was too heavy to bear.
Theodore brought him a new cover.
Pachomius was angry :
" Theodore, what a great injustice you have done.
Do you want me to give bad example to my brothers ?
They will say : Abba Pachomius has an easier life
than the rest of his brothers."
Theodore took off the cover

and brought an old used one,
worse than those the others had.

121   Pachomius was still ill during the 50 days of Eastertide.
Three days before he died
he gathered the brother superiors to him and said :
" You see that I am going to the Lord
who created me and gathered us together, to do his will.
Now then decide together
the one you wish to be your father."
No one answered because of their sorrow,
thinking how miserable they would be after his departure,
like sheep without their shepherd.
Pachomius said to Abba Horsiesios :
" Speak with them and find out what it is they desire."
They answered :
" We do not know. It is between you and the Lord.
You yourself choose, and we will obey."
Pachomius said to them :
" The Lord has made known to me that it is Petronios,
father of the monastery of Tsmine.
I think that he too is ill, but if he lives
he is your father."

122   Then he turned to Theodore and spoke to him :
" If the Lord visits me, do not leave my body
in the place where it will be buried."
This was because he was afraid
that a tomb would be built for his body
as was done for the holy martyrs.
And he added :
" Attention, Theodore ! If the brothers are careless,
you are to stir them up to the law of God.
You will be the voice of God for them."

Theodore said : " I understand."
But in his heart he was hesitant and wondered what he meant.
Then Pachomius said to him :
" Courage, Theodore, not only for what I am saying
but for what you are thinking in your heart."
And Theodore answered him with tears : " It is well."

123   After that, Pachomius said nothing more
and was unconscious for a little while.
Then he made three signs of the cross with his hand,
and suddenly gave up his spirit.
It was 9 May, 346, at 4 in the afternoon.
Theodore placed his hands on the eyes of Pachomius
in order to close them
as Joseph did for Jacob.   Gen 46. 3,4
All the brothers were in tears.
They moved forward to kiss the mouth of their Father
and all his holy body.

In the evening they placed the body in front of the altar.
All night, the brothers made Scripture readings and prayers for him.
After the morning Office they prepared for the burial
as they did for all the brothers,
and they offered the Eucharist for him.
They carried him to the mountain, singing psalms,
and buried him in the same way as all the brothers.
As they returned sadly, many of the brothers said to one another :
" Today we are orphans."

That night, Theodore with three brothers
raised the body from the grave
and reburied it elsewhere, with that of Abba Paphnouti.
And even now, no one knows the place.

Pachomius was 60 years old when he died.

He had been a monk since the age of 21,
remaining 39 years in the monastic life.
God saw he had mortified his flesh in everything
so as to do his will,
and he willed to give him rest.
He took him to himself
without permitting him to reach such a great age
that he would be weaker than he wanted.

Brothers were sent for Abba Petronios
and brought him back sick.
He died in July after appointing Abba Horsiesios
to be Father in his place.

124   Later in the year, Theodore was sent to Alexandria
with a letter for Archbishop Athanasius
concerning the death of Pachomius.

Theodore announces the death of Pachomius to Antony

122   Theodore took some brothers with him
to go and announce the death of Pachomius to Antony,
on the mountain of Tilog, in his hermitage of Pispir.
After a long and difficult journey, they found Antony
lying weak because of his advanced age.
When he understood that the brothers of Tabennisi were there,
he asked one of those with him to lift him up.
His brothers were surprised, because he was so old and weak,
but he walked out to meet the brothers from Tabennisi
and embraced them.
Then Theodore took him by his right hand
and Zachaeus by his left hand,
and they walked with him back to his cell.
They prayed and sat down.
Antony's face was as joyful as that of an angel.
He said :

" My brothers, do not be sad at the death of Pachomius
the just one.
You are now his body and have his spirit.
I had longed to see him during his life
but perhaps I was not worthy.
He gathered souls around him
to offer them holy to the Lord.
He has proved that he was superior to us
and that the cenobitic life is the true apostolic life."
Theodore answered politely :
" But you, the last of the prophets,
you are more praiseworthy than we."

Then Abba Zachaeus thoughtlessly said :
" Surely you are deceiving us.
If the cenobitic life is superior,
why have you not followed it ?
We know that you are perfect.
While he lived, our Father never stopped speaking to us
constantly about you."

147   Antony said to him :
" I am going to convince you, little Zachaeus (he was a short man).
When I became a monk
there was no community on earth where I could go and live.
There were only a few people
who used to withdraw a little way outside their villages
and live alone.
That is why I became a hermit.
Later, Abba Pachomius
undertook the apostolic way of life   Acts 4.34-7
and he became the refuge for everyone fleeing the devil.
If now I wanted to begin a community
I would not be able to do it because I have not developed

the necessary qualities to lead men,
and if I entered into a community
I am too old to practise obedience as a novice.
So, I have chosen to remain as I am."

• Sylvanus and Solomon

There was a young man called Sylvanus.
He had become careless and laughed frequently.
Pachomius told him to go back home.
The young man wept and promised to be a good monk.
Then Pachomius was patient with him.

Pachomius went to pray.
He asked the Lord to give the young man the grace to repent.
Then he called an old monk, a very holy brother, Solomon.
He said to him :
" I am going to tell you a secret.
Sylvanus formerly committed a very grave sin.
It is difficult for him to be saved in the cenobitic life.
Will you give your soul for his
and carry the cross for him,
share in great self-denial with him,
until he is saved ?
He needs someone to encourage him all the time
by word and by example.
If you accept
I will tell him to follow you in all that you do."
Solomon said : "I accept."
Pachomius called Sylvanus and said to him :
"Here is your father in God.
All that he does, you will do.

If he sits down to eat, you will sit beside him.
You will do nothing without his permission."
Sylvanus replied :
" I will do all that you tell me.
Only help me to save my soul."

And so they worked together making mats
and they fulfilled the fasts and the prayers regularly.
The young man obeyed in everything as he was commanded.
He would not eat even a vegetable leaf without asking.
And so he was humble and meek,
and kept his mouth shut.

One day Pachomius said to the brothers :
" I am going to tell you a secret of God.
Among you there is one who has become a new man.
His purity of heart has become perfect
thanks to the fruits of the Holy Spirit.
All that he does is done in the fear of the Lord.
Because of his purity
the Holy Spirit has filled him completely."
For three years the brothers tried to find out
the name of the man who was perfect.
Then Pachomius said that it was Sylvanus.
They were astonished because they scorned him.
The other monks came to Pachomius to say :
" It is not possible."
Then Pachomius explained to them :
" There is no one like him among you for his patience,
for knowledge of the Scriptures, for observances.
There are some stronger than he among you
but for purity of heart he is superior to all of you.
It is the grace of God that has done this
because he has killed his bad actions with a sharp knife.

There are two ways of defeating the enemy :
You can tie his hands and feet
or you can cut his throat.
You have overcome the devil by tying him up
but you still have to cut his throat.
The least carelessness on your part and he can go free.
Sylvanus has attacked the devil with a sharp knife ;
he bears everything in the spirit of the martyrs.
He always has death before his eyes
so that he will get to heaven.
Because of that he is a temple of the Holy Spirit.
And now you, little and great, watch well what he does,
for he does it all in the Holy Spirit.
You, Solomon, were his father in the past.
Now, it is he who is your father
because of the progress he has made."

THE MONK WITH A GRUDGE

In the time of Abba Eboneh,
one of the monks was unwilling to forgive a Brother.
So, Abba Eboneh took him to Tabennisi, to Pachomius,
our respected Father, a great friend of God.
Pachomius spoke these words to the Brother who held a grudge. *
Other older Fathers were there, listening with great pleasure.

Pachomius began thus:

> May the peace of God be with you.
> May the blessing of God and the blessing of all the saints
>   come down on us.
> May we all come to salvation. Amen.

Then he said to the monk :

1	My son : listen and be wise:	Prov 23.19
	accept the true teaching.	Sir 16.24
	There are Two Ways.	Didache 1-6
	You have the choice:	
	keep your bitter heart,	
	or start learning how to act as God desires.	

---

* To bear a grudge is to be bitter against someone who has done us a wrong.
When we keep bitterness like this in our heart we cannot forgive.

Follow the example of our fathers before us

Be able to obey God like **Abraham**.

2   Abraham left his own country to go to a strange land.
While there he lived in tents in the land
God said he would give him
But for him it was a strange land.   Heb 11.9
Abraham did as God said and humbled himself before him.
That is why God promised to give him many descendants.
God tested him : he asked for his son Isaac.
Abraham had courage. He gave his son to God.   Gen 22
For that, God called him his friend.   Jas 2.23

3   Copy the example of **Isaac** : he had a pure heart.
He did what his father said
and let himself be taken and given to God in sacrifice,
like a gentle lamb.

4   Copy the example of **Jacob**.
He humbled himself, he obeyed, he was patient.
Then Jacob was filled with light   Gen 32.30,31
and he saw God, the Father of the whole world.
God gave him the name Israel.   Gen 35.9,10

5   Again, copy the example of **Joseph**.
He too obeyed. He was a wise man.   Gen 39-41
Fight to keep your body pure and to be a servant for others :
you will rule in the Kingdom of heaven.

Up ! Do not stay with the dead.

6   My son, do good deeds like the friends of God.   Heb 6.12
Do not sleep : act !
And make your neighbour do good deeds,
for you have made yourself responsible for him.   Prov 6.1-6
Get up ! Do not stay with the dead,
and Christ will give you light   Eph 5.14
and grace will flower in you.   2 Cor 4.16,17

7   Yes, you will discover all God's good things
but for that you have to be patient.
The saints took pride in doing this
so they were given all that God had promised.   Heb 6.15
By patience you will become part of God's army.
You can be certain
that you will be given the eternal crown of glory.   1 Pet 5.4

8   When a thought keeps troubling you,
be patient,
waiting for God to give you back your peace.
    When you fast,
do not give way to your hunger.
    When you want to pray
stay in your room with no one but God.   Mt 6.6
    Be of one heart with your Brothers.
    Be completely pure, master of your thoughts,
master of your body, master of your heart.
    Keep your head low, your heart humble.
    Be gentle in the time of anger.

9   When a bad thought is a cross to you
do not be downhearted but keep your strength of purpose
saying : They came round me like bees !
In the name of the Lord I crushed them.   Ps 118.11,12
At once God will come to your help.
With him you will drive them from you.
You will be strong in heart,
the glory of the Lord will go with you
and you will be filled to your heart's desire.   Is 58.11
For the ways of the Lord are humility of heart and gentleness.
It is said : Whom shall I take note of ?
It is the one who is humble and lowly in spirit.   Is 66.2
If you walk in the ways of the Lord   Ps 127.1
he will watch over you and give you strength.
He will fill you with knowledge and wisdom.

The Lord will always keep you in mind.
He will keep you safe from the Spirit of Evil.
And on the day of your death he will give you his pea*ce*.

My son, do not sleep !

10   My son, I ask you to be watchful
and not to sleep.
Those who hate you watch for you in secret :
they are the evil spirits.
They walk hand in hand,
two, three or more together.
These are the bad things they can make you do :
You give way to fear and so you do not keep faith ;
you do not say what is true, and then you act deceitfully ;
you love money too much and try to get more and more ;
you do not keep to your word,
you act deceitfully with others, and become full of envy :
all these go together.
You want to look important
and at the same time you overeat.
You act like a prostitute and become impure in what you do.
You are against others and you become sad.

So when these evil spirits start living in someone
how unhappy that person is !
They are stronger than he and keep him from God.
Such a soul may fight on all sides
but the evil spirits own him
and in the end he is taken from God for ever,

*Listen t*o my experience

11   My son, do what I say. Do not be careless,
give your eyes no sleep, your eyelids no rest,
so that you may run free like a gazelle from the nets. Prov 6.4,5

My son, from the time when I was a child
all the evil spirits have attacked me frequently.
When I was in the desert they troubled me so much
that I nearly lost heart. I was saying to myself :
I am not able to drive back the attacks of the Spirit of Evil.
In fact he troubled me in every possible way.
When I was with other men
he made his evil spirits flame out against me and attack ;
when I stayed by myself he pained me with unholy words.
Many times my heart was full of grief.
I turned from side to side and had no peace.
I ran to God with tears and humility.
I fasted and took no sleep.
Then the chief of the spirits, and all of them,
became feeble before me.
God filled me with his fire
and all at once I felt his strength.
Yes, God is good and lets the sons of men see
that he is powerful and can help them.

Be small in your own eyes

12   My son, do not ever scorn anyone.
When you see someone given honour,
do not say : That man already has his reward.   Mt 6.5
Keep yourself from such a thought, for it is very bad.
The man who has praise only for himself
and looks down on his brother
is hateful to God.
The one who says to himself that he is somebody great
when he is nothing,
he is in error and will not see it.   Gal 6.3
Who can help him in his pride ?
When he says : ' There is no one equal to me '
he makes himself like God.

He will soon hear God say :
" You will go down to hell, you will be put in with the dead,
your flesh will be diseased
and worms will be all over your body."   Is 14.11
On the other hand, one who can be humble
is his own judge.
He says : 'My sins are greater than those of any one else.'
He judges no one and looks down on no one
Who are you to judge a servant that is not yours ?
The Lord can certainly lift up
anyone who has fallen.   Rom 14.4
Keep watch over yourself, my son, look down on no one.
Taste all the virtues and keep them.

13   Are you a stranger ? Stay by yourself.
Request nothing from the people of that country
and mind your own business.
Are you poor ? Do not be downhearted.
Let it not be said of you :
To be poor is to be called evil
in the mouth of the godless.   Sir 13.24

Look to God for your food

And let it not be said to you :
'You take no food so you will go out of your mind
and will say something bad
about your superior and father.'   Is 8.21
Watch when you have not enough food
that you are not overcome by the Spirit of Evil.
Do not be downhearted but be faithful.
God has certainly something ready for you in secret.

Have in mind the prophet **Habakkuk** in Judea
and **Daniel** in Chaldea.

There was a distance of a day's journey between them
and Daniel had been thrown down a pit to be food for the lions.
But the prophet Habakkuk took him his meal.   Dan 14.33-38
Keep in mind **Elijah** in the desert
and the widow of Sarephtah.   1 Kgs 19
At that time there was no rain and no food.
This woman was suffering the pains of hunger
but she was not faint-hearted:
she kept on and had her reward.
God gave, as he promised:
she and her son had all the food they needed.

If you give bread when you have plenty of it
are you being truly good ?
And if you are downhearted when you are in need
you are not truly poor in spirit.
But the Bible says of the saints
that they are in need of everything,
they go through all sorts of troubles,
and they are ill-used.   Heb 11.37
But they are proud
of having to undergo these things.   Rom 5.3

Continue the fight against evil

Go on with the fight, as the Scriptures say.
Then you will be free.
This is what the Apostle Paul says :
No one should judge you
for the things which you eat and drink,
or about feasts or a new moon or a sabbath.
All that is only a shadow of what is to come.
It is Christ who truly is.   Col 72.16,17
14   Repeat the words of God all day.
Do not give way to feeling tired.

Thank God for everything he sends.   Eph 5.20
Run from the praise of men.
Love the Brother who, because he loves and respects God,
points out your errors.
Take what is good in others,
then you will be able to be good to everyone.

Go right on with the righteous God

Keep on wi*th your work.*
When you speak, say nothing that can be blamed.
Do not take one step forward and another back,
so that God may not find you hateful.   Rev 3,16; Jas 1.6,7
The prize is for the one who runs right on to the end.
More and more, follow what God says
and God will give you salvation.   Mt 10.22

15   When you are among your Brothers
do not give way to saying and doing things
to make them laugh.
Shadrach, Meshach and Abednego would not agree
to the foolishness of Nebuchadnezzar.   Dan 3
That is why the king's fine music
and the good meals at his table
could not make them do evil.
So, the fire which was more than 20 foot high
could not burn them.
They did not bend to one who was bent
but remained upright with the one who is upright, that is, God.
For this reason God helped them
and they mastered those who were against them.
Daniel in his turn did not do wrong as the Chaldeans wanted.
He went on watching before God
and making his prayer at the fixed times.   Dan 6
So he 'shut the mouths of lions'.   Heb 11.33

16   And now, my son, if you hope in God
   he will be your help in the time of trouble.
   Yes, anyone who comes to God has first to believe this :
   God is
   and he rewards those who seek him.   Heb 11.6
   These words were written for us. Why ?
   So that all of us, little and great, may have faith in God
   and fight on by fasting, prayers and other good practices.
   Even when your tongue is dry because you are fasting,
   God will not forget it.
   Quite the opposite : when the hour of death comes
   you will be given a reward for it all.

   Only, make yourself small in everything.
   Do not put in your word at once
   even if you know all about what is being said.
   Do not, little by little,
   develop the habit of saying hard things against the others.

   Bearing hard things with joy

Joyfully undergo any troubles.
If you knew the honour
which is the reward of undergoing troubles
you would not ask God to take them away.
Yes, when you are weeping in your prayer,
and when you are watching long hours for God's help,
that is of more value to you than to let yourself get soft
and be made a prisoner.
As the prophet **Baruch** said to his Hebrew brothers :
Man, what are you doing here in Babylon ?
It is because you would not undergo the test
and because you are not right with God.
So you have grown old in a strange land   Bar 3.10
That is why, Brother, you should not relax.

17   It may be that there are times when you do not remember,
     but those who hate you do not sleep.
     Night and day they remember to set traps for you.
     So do not look for honours,
     and then they will not be taken from you
     which would be joy for those who hate you !
     Instead, try to be humble.
     For whoever makes himself high will be made low,
     and whoever makes himself lowly
     will be made high.   Mt 23.12

     If you are not able to go on by yourself,
     join another who is living by the Gospel of Christ.
     With him you will go forward.
     Open your ears,
     or do what another says who has his ears open.
     Be strong and be called **Elijah**,
     or do what the strong one says and be called **Elisha**.
     Elisha did what Elijah said
     and for that God gave him a double share of the spirit of Elijah
     for his heritage.   2 Kgs 2.9,15

18   If you prefer to live among others,
     copy the example of **Abraham. Lot, Moses, Samue**l.
     If you wish to live in the desert,
     all the prophets took the way there before you. Be like them :
     they were wandering over deserts and mountains,
     in the valleys, and in holes in the rocks,   Heb 11.38
     deep in trouble, pain and suffering.
     Again, the prophet Isaiah says :
     You give shade for those dry with heat
     and courage for the cruelly ill-used
     and they bless you.   Isaiah 25.4
     To the thief on the cross, the one who spoke a word,

Jesus gave forgiveness of his sins
and took him to paradise.   Lk 23. *40-43*

   Keep your body pure

Such honours are for you if you stay strong under testing.
Fight against the Spirit of Evil
who hopes to lead your body into sin.
Fight against the spirit of pride and all other bad desires.
War against evil passions, the suggestions of the devil,
in order not to fall.
Then Jesus will give you the reward he has promised.
Keep from being careless.
Carelessness is the mother of all the vices.

19   My son, run from the bad desires of the body.
    They cloud the mind
    and they stop you from coming to the knowledge
    of the secrets of God.   Mt 13.11
    They make you a stranger to the words of the Holy Spirit,
    and you will not be able to carry the cross of Christ,
    or keep your heart's attention on praising God.
    Do not eat more than you need
    or you will not be able to taste the things of God.
    Keep your body pure :
    impure acts anger God and his angels.

20   My son, turn towards God and love him.
    Run from the Evil Spirit and scorn him.
    May God turn his face toward you
    and give you the heritage of Judah the son of Jacob.
    Here is that blessing :
    'Judah, your mother will praise you,
    your hands will be on the neck of those that hate you,
    and the sons of your father will be your servants. '   Gen *49.8*

Watch out for *pride*

Keep away from pride
for it is the beginning of every evil,
and the beginning of pride is to stay away from God.
Then your heart becomes hard.
On the other hand, if you take care about this
your resting place will be the heavenly Jerusalem.
If the Lord loves you and gives you glory and honour
keep from becoming proud because of it.
Do the opposite : stay humble
and you will go on living in the glory that God has given you.

Be on the watch at all times

Be watchful, take care of what you do.
'Happy is the servant
whose master finds him watching',   Mt 24. 46-47
and that one will go joyfully into the Kingdom of Heaven.
The Holy Book says also :
The friends of the bridegroom will love him
because they have seen him
keeping watch over his vineyard.   Song of Songs 7.11,12

21   My son, be merciful, and faithful in all things,
for it is written :
Do your best to offer yourself before God for his approval
like a man who gladly lets the quality of his work be inspected,
like a workman who has no fear of shame.   2 Tim 2.15
Go before God
like a farmer who plants seed and reaps the corn,
and you will gather God's goods in your storehouse.
Do not make prayers for all to see like false men.   Mt 6.5
Put aside your foolish desires.
Do what you do for God
and so act for your own salvation.

Be lion-hearted

If a passion springs up in you : a love of money,
envy, or hate, or any of the other passions,
watch out !
Have the heart of a lion, a strong heart.
Fight against these desires.
Put them to death as was done once
to those old kings of Palestine :   Sihon, Og and the others,
who were put to death.   Deut 31.3-4
May King Jesus, God's only Son whom he loves,
fight for you, and may the towns of those that hate you
become your heritage.
But this is on two conditions :
put all pride far from you, and have strength of purpose
.

Look :
when **Joshua** son of Nun was strong in the fight,   Josh 2.10,11
God gave his enemies into his hands.
If you are feeble-hearted
you become a stranger to the law of God,
you look out for good reasons to do nothing,
you are no longer truly alive.
Be strong-hearted and cry out :
" Who can separate us from the love of God ?"   Rom 8.35
And say : "Though my body is on the way to death,
my soul is made new every day.   2 Cor 4.16

Look for the honour that God gives

22   When you are in doubt, fight with these weapons :
prayer, fasting, and acts of self-control.
When you are among men, be wise as snakes
and simple as doves.   Mt 10.16
If someone curses you, bear with him joyfully.
Hope that God will do for you what is best,

but you yourself must not curse anyone.
For a person is the image of God.
It is God himself who said :
One who honours me, I will honour,
and of one who says ill of me,
ill will be said of him.   1 Sam 2.30
If someone praises you, do not be happy about it.
Jesus has said : Unhappy are you when people speak well of you
but happy are you when they say things to you in anger
and drive you out from among them
and curse your very name as evil.   Lk 6.22-26

Look at our fathers **Barnabas and Paul**.
When they were honoured they were sad,
they tore their garments   Acts 14.14
as a sign that what the people were saying
was against God's honour. They scorned human glory.

When the apostles **Peter and John**
were taken before the Sanhedrin
the Jews cursed them and they came out rejoicing
because they had been thought good enough to be cursed
for the Lord's holy name.   Acts 5.41
Their hope was in the glory of heaven.

Run from earthly honours

23   You, my son, run from the soft life of this world.
Then you will be happy in the world to come.
Do not be careless, letting the days go by,
for then Death will come to you suddenly
and his servants, the faces of fear, come round you   *

---

* The faces of fear are the servants of death, Abaddon.   (Rev 9.7-11)

and cruelly take you off to their dark place
of terror, fear and pain.
Do not be sad when you are cursed by men :
be deeply sad when you sin —
this is the true curse —
and you go away bearing the wound of your sin.

24   From my heart I urge you
to scorn honours.
Pride is the Devil's own weapon.
It was with this arm of pride
that he worked his deceit against **Eve**.
He said to her :
"Take and eat the fruit of the tree
and your eyes will be opened
and you will be like gods."   Gen 3.5
She listened to him and thought it true.
She desired the glory of being like God
and her own human glory was taken away,
And you, if you go after the glory which comes from men
it will keep you from the glory which comes from God.

It was different for Eve.
No one had told her that the evil spirit would test her.
That is why the Word of God came,
and took flesh of the Virgin Mary
to free all the offspring of Eve.
But the saints of God who came before you
have given warning about this war, in the Sacred Scriptures.
So, my Brother, do not say :
" I have never heard of all this,
not yesterday nor the day before."
For it says in the Scriptures that :
Their voice goes out through all the world,
their words to the ends of the earth.   Ps 18.4

When bad things are said about you, thank God.

So, if you are praised, control your heart
and give the glory to God.
If you are cursed, thank God
that you are given the same heritage
as the Son of God and the friends of God.
Your Lord was said to be false,   Mt 27. 63
the prophets were said to be good for nothing
and others, foolish.
The more should we, who are dust and ashes,   Sir 10.9; 17.32
not be sad when we are cursed.
It is your way to life.
If you let yourself grow careless, then weep,
for in the Scriptures it says :
Those who grew up in purple
now lie in the dust,   Lam 4.5
because they were careless about the law of God
and went after their own changing desires.
So, my son, go weeping every hour before the Lord
for it is in the Scriptures :
Happy the man you have chosen
and brought into your holy house.
You have put a strong thought into his heart
in the valley of tears,
you made a place ready for him.   Ps 83.4-7

God is living in you, you should be living in him

25   Look for what is good everywhere, be without deceit.
Be like the gentle sheep.
They are fleeced but they say nothing.   Is 53.7
Do not go from place to place saying :
I will find God here, I will find him there.   Mt 24.23
God has said :
I am everywhere in heaven and on earth.   Jer 23.24

And again :
If you cross over water I am with you.
The waves will not swallow you.   Is 43.2
My son, you should realise that God is in you,
so that you may have life in him, in his law and his commands.
Look :
the thief was on the cross and he went into paradise,
but **Judas** was among the Apostles
and he handed his Lord over to those who hated him.
Rahab was a prostitute
and she was counted among the saints,   Jas 2.25
but see, **Eve** was in paradise,
and the Spirit of Evil led her into sin.   Gen 3
Job was on a dungheap,
and they say he was like his Lord,   Jas 5.11
but see, **Adam** was in God's garden
and he did not do as God commanded.
The angels were in heaven and God threw them out,   2 Pet 2.4
Elijah and **Enoch** were on earth,
but they were taken up to heaven.   2 Kgs 2.11; Heb 11.5

So we should see God in every place
and look for his help at all times.   Ps 104.4

*I*mitate *those who look to God*

Yes, look *to God like **Abraham*** :
he did what God said, he offered his son to God in sacrifice.
God called him 'friend'.   Jas 2.23
Look to God like **Joseph** :
he fought to stay pure   Gen 39.7-13
and he became ruler over his enemies.
Look to God like **Moses** :
he followed his Lord
and he made him Lawgiver

95

and let him see him as he is.   Ex 33.11
Daniel looked to God
and he gave him knowledge of secret things,
he kept him safe from the mouth of the lions.   Dan.1,17; 6.23
The **Three Young Men** looked to God
and he came to them in the burning fire.   Dan 3.49
Job went to God for help   Job 42.14
and God healed his wounds.
Susannah looked to God   Dan 13.1-63
and God kept her safe from the evil old men.
Judith looked to God,
and he was in the tent of Holofernes.   Jud 13.1-14
All of these looked to God
and God rescued them, these and many more.

26   So my son,
      how long will you be careless ?
      How careless will you be ?
      Last year you were careless. This year you are still careless.
      What you did yesterday, you do today.
      As long as you are careless
      you will not go forward.
      Be watchful, lift your heart,
      because you will have to go before the judgment seat of God.
      You will have to give an account
      of what you have done in secret and in public.   Rom 14.10,12

   Fight for God

   If you go where the battle is — God's battle —
   and the Spirit of God urges you on saying :
   'Do not go to sleep here because there are traps along the way',
   and if the Spirit of Evil says softly :
   ' What happened to you that other time ?' or:
   'Even if this or that comes of it, do not be sad',

then do not give in to his deceitful talk.
If you do, the Spirit of God will leave you
and you will be feeble and with no strength like **Samson**.
Samson opened his heart to **Delilah**.
That is why the Philistines put him in chains
and made him crush grain, and regret.   Judg 16..17-21
For you it will be the same :
they will chain you up and laugh at you.
They put out his eyes
and he was not able to see the way to the city.
So it will be for you.
For you, Delilah is the Spirit of Evil.
He has taken you by surprise
because you have not cared about the words of the Holy Spirit.

You have seen the error of **David**,
and he was a strong man.
He took the wife of Uriah.
Happily, he quickly regretted his sin.   2 Sam 11-12
You have seen **Job**'s sores.
He says to you : You have seen my troubles,
be fearful for yourself.   Job 6.21

Watch out for the Spirit of Evil

28   When a Brother says a harsh word to you,
      why do you get angry ?
      Why become like a beast to him ?
      Why do you not keep in mind
      that Christ died for you ?   Rom 5.8; 1 Cor 15.3
      But when the one who hates you, the Spirit of Evil,
      speaks softly in you ear,
      you give him a hearing.
      You open your heart to put poison in.
      Unhappy man !

That is the time to become like an angry beast,
or flare out and burn up all his deceit,
or feeling sick throw up all the evil
before the poison spreads all through you and you die.
Man, you did not put up with a little word
spoken by a Brother.
But when the one who hates you
comes to eat up your soul   1 Pet 5.8
what do you do ? You let him do it !
No, my friend, we should not have to be sad about you
because 'your hair will be cut off because of your actions,
when you should have a crown of gold. '   Is 3.24
So keep a watch on yourself,
put up gladly with the one who curses you,
be good to your Brother.
Have no fear of the troubles of this world.

29   Take in the words of the wise Paul when he says :
There are chains and beatings for us in Jerusalem,
but I do not have any questioning in my heart
about the way my life will end ;   Acts 20. 23-24
I am ready for death in Jerusalem
for the name of the Lord Jesus.   Acts 21.13

Your body is Christ's

You see, troubles and trials
did not stop the saints from going to the Lord.
So have courage and faith.
No more fear : it comes from the spirit of Evil.
Run after the example of the saints
and their strength of purpose.
My son, why do you run away from the Lord God
and straight into captivity —
why do you open you heart to the evil spirits ?

30   My son, keep away from shameful acts.   1 Thess 4.3

Do not dirty the parts of Christ's body.
Do not do what the evil spirits say.
Your body is Christ's.
Let it not become one
with the body of a prostitute.   1 Cor 6.15
Keep the pain of the punishment in mind.
Put before your eyes the judgment of God.
Run from every evil desire.
Put off the old man and his works,
clothe yourself in the new man.   Col 3.9
Keep in mind the fear of that judgment
when you will go out of your body.

31   My son, run to God,
     for he made you,
     and it was for you that he underwent those sufferings.
     For he said by the mouth of the Prophet Isaiah :
     I offered my back to the whips
     and my head to the blows.
     I did not turn my face away from the shame.   Is 50.6

Run from sin

     'O man, what is the good of going to Egypt
     to drink the waters of the Nile ? It is defiled.'   Jer 2.18
     What good is it for you to have these troubled thoughts
     so that you undergo all these pains ?
     It is better to turn back to the right way
     weeping over your sins.
     In the book of Isaiah it says :
     When he makes himself an offering for sin
     we shall see his offspring to the third generation.   Is 53.10
32   You have seen then, man, that wrongdoing is evil
     and that sin causes trouble and pain.
     Quick, man, run from your sin.

Keep death in your thoughts.
In the Scriptures it says this :
The wise man sees the evil and takes cover.   Prov 29.8
Have in mind that Moses preferred to be
with the ill-used people of God in their troubles
and not to profit from the pleasures of sin
which are quickly past and gone.   Heb 11.25
If you love to undergo the sufferings of the saints
they will be your friends.
They will be your go-between with God
and God will give you all your right requests
because you took up your cross and followed your Lord.
33   Do not look for high honour from men
and God will shelter you when strange winds blow.
He will give you a place in his great city,
the heavenly Jerusalem.
Test all things and keep what is good.   1 Thess 5.21
Do not treat any other with scorn:
that one is the image of God.

Keep in mind the day of judgment

Keep an eye on yourself while you are young
so that you may be able to keep watch over your behaviour
when you are old.
If you do not,
the eyes of everyone will be on you on the day of judgment
and you will know shame and regret when they say :
We thought all the time you were a sheep
and here we see you are a wolf !   Didache 16.3
Now you shall go into the mouth of hell
deep in the earth and far from God.   Is 14.15
Oh, what a fall !
In the world you went about praised
like one of the great and good,

and when you come to Judgment Day
you are found naked
and all see your sins.   2 Cor 5.3
You are truly hateful to God and to man.
Unhappy you, then.
Where will you turn your face ?
Will you open your mouth ?
To say what ?
Because of your sins your soul is as black
as a goat-hair shirt.
What will you do then ?
Go weeping ? There will be none to take note of your tears.
Pray ? No one will hear your prayers,
for those to whom you are handed over are without pity.
How unhappy you will be, hearing the fearful words :
'Sinners, go to hell.   Ps 9. 17
Go far from me, you cursed ones,
into the eternal fire which is ready for the Evil One
and his angels.   Mt 25.41
I shall cut off all the evil-doers
from the Lord's city.'   Ps *100.8*

God is your helper

34   Now, my son, look carefully to the ordering of your life
     while you are still on earth.   1 Pet 1.17
     Go on with the thought that you yourself are nothing;
     follow the Lord in all things.
     So on the day of judgment you will be able to be confident.
     Let others in the world see you as good for nothing
     and on the day of judgment you will discover
     that you are dressed in glory.
     Give your heart to no one for your soul's pleasure,
     but give all your cares to the Lord
     and he will support you.   Ps 54.22

Look at **Elijah** by the brook Kerith :
he put his trust in God
and God gave him food by means of the raven.   1 Kgs 17.5-6

35   Keep far away from useless desires
for they have wounded many and led them into sin.
Do not take a young boy for a friend.
Do not run after a woman.
Run from pleasing bodily touches
for love for a friend quickly flares up like a flame.
Do not chase after any flesh
because a hard stone upon iron
makes a spark fly out and cause much destruction.
Run at all times to the Lord,
sit in his shadow,
for he who is living under the care of the Most High
and in the shadow of the God of heaven
will never be moved.   Ps 91.1
Keep the Lord and the heavenly Jerusalem in your thoughts
and God will bless you and take you into his glory.

Seek after peace and be holy

36   Be watchful in overcoming your body and your heart.
Seek after peace and be holy   Heb 12.14
— the two go together.
Then you will see God.
Do not be against anyone,
because he who is against his brother is against God,
and he who has peace with his brother has peace with God.
Do you not yet know
that nothing is better than peace,
which makes each one love his brother ?
You may be pure and free from all other sin
but if you hate your brother you are a stranger to God.
Yes, Scripture says :

Seek after peace and be pure
for the two go together.   Heb 12.14
And again :
If I had the faith needed to move mountains,
and if I did not have true love,
it would be no use to me.   1 Cor 13.2-3
To love is to build up.   1 Cor 8.1
How can you become clean if you want to be dirty ?   Sir 34.4
If you keep hatred in your heart or are against anyone
where is your purity ?
The Lord says to us by the mouth of Jeremiah :
" You say words of peace to your brother
but in your heart you hate him."   Jer 9.8
Or put simply : you keep bad thoughts in your heart against him.
Then God says : " Will I not be angry with one like that ?"
It is as though God says :
" The man who is against his brother
is a man who has not the faith
and such people walk in darkness.
They do not come to the light."   Eph 4.17-18
The one who hates his brother
walks in darkness and has no knowledge of God
because his hate blinds his eyes
and he does not see God's image in his brother.

Jesus says to you : Love those who hate you.

37   The Lord has commanded us :
Love those who are against you,
and pray for those who curse you,
and do good to those who are cruel to you.   Mt 5.44
So, when we hate one another
we are in great danger.
The others are our brothers,
one with us and parts of the one body.

They are sons of God, branches of the true Vine. Jn 15.5
They are sheep of the Holy Spirit,
gathered together by Jesus the true shepherd. Jn 10.14
The only Son of God gave his life for us,
the Living Word Jn 1.1-4
underwent these sufferings for so great a work.
And you, when you are full of envy, pride, desire,
and without respect,
you oppose the work that Jesus has done.
The Evil One has caught you in his trap
to make you a stranger to God.
What will you say to Christ ?
He will say to you : " You hate your brother ?
Then it is I whom you hate !" Mt 25.40,46
And you will go away to eternal punishment
because you do not love your brother.
But your brother will go into eternal life
because, for love of Jesus,
he made himself small before you.
38 So let us use the time we have in this life
to search out how to right this wrong.

Love covers many sins

Beloved friends, let us turn to the Gospel,
the true law of God the Christ.
He says :
Do not judge others and God will not judge you,
forgive and God will forgive you. Lk 6.37
If you do not forgive
you will not be forgiven.
If you are angry with your brother,
get ready for the punishment of your errors,
your wrong-doing, your impure acts —
even those you have done in secret —

your evil thoughts, your bad words, your wrong desires.
You will have to give an account of all these
before the judgment seat of Christ.
There the whole world will see you.
The angels and all the heavenly host will be there, sword in hand.
They will force you to give an account
and make a statement of your sins.
You will be covered in shame, you will foul your garments.
Fear will shut your mouth.
You will not have a word to say.
Unhappy man,
of how many things you will have to give an account !
Your impure acts have diseased your soul,
the desires of your eyes and your bad thoughts
make you sad and full of trouble.
Your body is soiled
by what goes out of your mouth :   Mt 15.17-20
bad rough and foolish words,
envy, hate, pride, false and angry disrespectful talk.
You have laughed at your brother,
cursed and judged him, the image of God.
And by giving way to the pleasures of the stomach
you have cut yourself off from the riches of heaven.
For all these things that you have done
you will have to make payment   1 Pet 4.5
because of your lack of love for your brother,
and you did not order things rightly in the love of God.
Love covers many sins :   1 Pet 4.8
have you never heard that ?
'So will your heavenly Father do to you
if you do not every one of you forgive your brother
from your heart. '   Mt 18.35
Yes, it is certain, your Father in heaven
will not forgive your sins.

39   Much loved Brothers, you know
that we have put on Christ,   Rom 13.14 ; Gal 3.27
who is good and the friend of men and women.
Let us not put him off again through our evil doings.
We have made the promise to God of our purity
and our monastic life.
Let us do what we have said we would do,
that is : fasting, continuous prayer,
keeping our body and our heart pure.
If we have offered to him a pure life,
let him not see us unfaithful
in one way or another.
Yes, it is said,
They have acted shamelessly in a number of ways.   Ez 16.26
My Brothers, let no one discover us doing this sort of thing.
Let us not be worse than other people.
We have offered ourselves to be disciples of Christ.
Let us go without certain pleasures :
it is a good way to keep purity.
Now is the time for the fight.
Let us not run away.
If we run away we may become slaves of sin.
We have been set as a light for the world.   Mt 6.14
Let us keep silence
for many have come to salvation because they kept silent.

41   Brothers, attend to what you do.
Let us not be without mercy to one another
or God will be without mercy to us at the judgment.

The grief of Christ

Yes, even if we keep our virginity,
and choose to live in poverty and solitude,
God will still say to us :

" Give me back my goods with interest."   Mt 25.27
Angrily he will say to us :
" Where is your robe for the bridal-feast ?   Mt 22. 11,12
Where is your shining light ?   Mt 5.15.16; 25.10-12
If you are my son,
where is my love and honour ?
If you are my servant, where is my respect ?   Mal 1.6
42   Did you lack anything when I was on earth ?   Lk 22.35
Did I not give you the blessing of my body and blood
as the food of life ?
Did I not taste death because of you,
to give you salvation ?
I gave you knowledge of the heavenly secrets
to make you my brother and my friend.
I gave you the power to crush underfoot snakes and scorpions
and all the strength of the Evil One.   Lk 10.19
More than one remedy I gave you
to make your life healthy and bring you to salvation.
I have given you the armour that I put on here in the world,
that is, my wonder-working.   Jn 14.12
With that you are able to overcome Goliath, that is, the Devil.
Why have you become a stranger to me ?
Now, what is it that you lack ?
You have not been careful of what you do.
That is the only reason why you are separated from God
for ever. "
43   Now my son, that is why
you have to obey the Lord's command.
If we do not forgive one another
we shall hear these hard words and more still.

Learning the ways of God

We must attend to ourselves
and recognise God's gifts.

107

They will be a help to us at our death.
They will be our guide in the hard and fearful fight
against the Evil One.
They will be the power which will make us pass over
from death to life.

First, God gives us faith in him and knowledge of him
so that we can go on driving away doubt.
Then he gives us good sense and makes us wise
so that we can recognise the Devil's scheme
and hate it and run from it.
We have been learning about prayer, fasting and self-control
to calm our body and keep our passions in check.
Purity of heart and watchful care have been given to us :
through them, God is living in us.
He makes us able to bear wrong done to us
and to be gentle.
If we use all these things
we shall have the glory of God for our inheritance.

44   God gives us love and peace.
They are powerful in the fight against the Spirit of Evil.
He is not able to approach where they are.
God gives us the command to use joy in our fight against sadness.
We have been learning to be good
and to give ourselves generously.
We have been given holy and continuous prayer
which makes the soul full of light.
We have been given the ability to be open and simple
and this overcomes hate.
Scripture tells us we should not make accusations
against others   Mt 7.1
and this keeps us all from saying what is not true.
Saying what is not true is a shameful error.
If we do not judge we shall not be judged

on the day of judgement.
We have been given the strength to undergo pain and trouble
and not grow *weary.*

Avoid drinking wine

45   The Fathers, in fact, went all through their lives
fasting from food and drink.
They desired to put to death the evil in themselves,
in order to gain purity of life.
Above all they did not let themselves get used to drinking wine.
Wine makes even the wise to turn away from the right road.
Much wine makes the body ill
and causes us to sin.
Then our life bears no fruit and our actions are bad.
When someone loves drinking he never has enough
and it clouds his mind and darkens it.
He loses all knowledge of the difference between good and evil.
He talks foolishly.
True joy comes from not causing grief to the Holy Spirit
by becoming like animals.   Eph 4.19,30
The prophet Isaiah has said :
' The priest and the prophet are made foolish by wine',   Is 28.7
and the Book of Proverbs says again :
' A man who drinks much
does not know what he is doing or saying.
And he falls into sin.'   Prov 20.1
Wine is a good thing if you drink only a little.
If you drink a lot your eyes will not see clearly
and you will behave badly.
That is why all those who are learning to be disciples of Jesus
should not drink much wine.
46   In fact the knowledge they had of the great damage
that is caused by wine made the fathers not drink it at all,
or a very little if they were ill.

One day the apostle Paul gave Timothy an order
to drink some wine.
But it was because this disciple worked hard
and he had a bad stomach and was frequently ill.   1 Tim 5.23
What shall I say to a man who is young and strong
and full of the fire of passion ?
I fear to say to him : "Never drink wine "
because that is displeasing to many these days
and one or other, unmindful of his salvation,
may say something bad of me.
Yet it is wise to be watchful,
and it is useful to control ourselves even in good things.
In this way you will take your ship safely
into the harbour of salvation
and you will be able to taste all the good things of heaven.

Humility is the greatest strength

47   More than all this,
we have been given humility.
It keeps all God's gifts safe.
It is that great and holy strength which the Son of God put on
when he came into the world.
Humility is a strengthening wall
and a storehouse for God's gifts,
protective clothing to keep us safe in the fight,
and healing for every wound.
At the time of the Exodus
the Hebrews made soft linens and things of gold
for the Tabernacle.
But at God's order they covered it all over
with a tent of goat's hair.   Ex 26. 7-11,14
Humility is least prized among men
but in the eyes of God it is of great value.
If we obtain it, we shall be able to crush underfoot

all the power of the Evil One.

God himself has said :" Who is the man to whom I will look ?

He that is humble and gentle.   Is 66.2

Living today is hard

These days we are seriously short of some important things.

People say much about themselves,

they look for honours and pleasure,

they over-eat, go to bed with anyone,

and are full of pride.

The young nowadays do not do what the old ones say.

The old now do not love the young.

Each one does what pleases him.

Now is the time to cry aloud with the prophet Micah :   Mic 7.1,2

" Unhappy is my soul ! There are no upright men on earth.

The good men are not in Christ. Everyone crushes his neighbour."

Brothers whom I love, continue with the fight.

Life is short.

The bad old days are over now, *

but fathers are not teaching their children.

The children do not do what their fathers say.

There are no more virgins.

On all sides the holy men are dead.

There are no good mothers and widows.

So we are all like orphans.

People who have no power are crushed ;

blows fall on the heads of the poor.

In a little time God will be angry.

He will punish us and no one will be able to help us.

All this is because we have not mastered our evil desires.

---

* After the Emperor Constantine became a Christian there was no longer
  at that time the opportunity for martyrs to give their lives for Christ.
  This was around the year 312

50   God has ready for us a kingly crown and a seat of honour,
the door of his kingdom is open.
He has said :
To him who overcomes
I will give some of the sacred manna.   Rev 2.7
If we fight and overcome our bad desires
we shall be kings eternally.
But if we are overcome, we shall mourn
and be weeping bitter tears.

Let us keep watch with a good heart

Let us fight against ourselves in all the ways we are able.
Let us put to death our bad desires
and we shall become new men, in purity.
Let us love others, and we shall be friends of Christ,
who is the friend of all men and women.

51   We have given our oath to God that our life will be monastic,
which is to love,
and for that we keep virginity not only of body
but the virginity that is a weapon against every sin.
In the Gospel it says :
Some virgins were guests at a wedding-feast
but some of them did not do what they should have done.
So they had to stop at the door and were sent back.
The others kept watch courageously :
they went in after the bridegroom to the feast.
May everyone go in there *for ever.*

Money is a trap

52   The love of money means loss of peace.
Riches are like the bait the fisherman puts on his hook.
If you desire to be rich you are caught on the hook.
So as to heap up gold or silver you will trade selfishly,
get the wealth you desire by being violent or full of deceit,

or you will over-work, and have no time for the work of God.
Keep in mind the words of the Gospel:
'Foolish man ! This night you will have to give up your soul.
Then, who will get what you have kept for yourself ? '   Lk 12.20
And keep in mind this word of the psalm :
A man amasses riches and does not know
who will have them.   Ps 39.6

53   My friend, fight bad desires and say :
I will act like Abraham who said :
" I swear by the Most High who made heaven and earth,
I will not take anything that is yours,
not a thread, not a shoe-string."   Gen 14.22-3
Those were great goods for a poor stranger.
Moses said to the Hebrews :
The Lord loves the stranger.
He gives him food and clothing.   Deut *10.18*

Work to help others

God commands us to work,
not to have a soft living but to have enough to help the poor.
'Keep in mind this word of God :
Your storehouses and everything in them
will be cursed. '   Deut 28.17
About gold and silver we have the words of the Lord :
' Your gold and silver have rusted
because you have not used them.
The rust proves you guilty
and it will eat into your flesh like fire. '   Jas 5.3
And Jeremiah says :
' First place goes to the just man
who has no false gods ',   Letter of Jeremiah 72
for he sees they are without value.
So, before the Lord comes for you,
cleanse yourself of the curse of money,

for you have set your hope on God
as it says in the Scriptures:
May your heart be pure and upright before God.   1 Kgs 8.*61*

A new life in Christ

54   Indeed you have taken God as your suppor*t*,
     you have become dear to him,
     you have set out with all your heart
     to walk according to God's commands.
     May God be with you.
     May your springs of water become rivers
     and your rivers become a sea.   (see Is 48.18)
     Yes, you work hard to get control over yourself.
     God makes his light shine before you :
     let the gospel light of his Spirit be reflected from you.
     May God give you the strength of his saints.
     May no false god be found among you.
     May your feet rest on the neck of the prince of darkness.
     May you see Michael the chief of the good spirits
     at your right side.   Jos 5.13,14
     Pharaoh and his army will fall into the sea,
     and you will be able without danger
     to go with your people across the salt sea,
     that is, this life on earth.   Ex *14.22*

Stay ever watchful

65   Now I again urge you to keep your strength of purpose.
     When a person is no longer watchful
     that pleases the Spirit of Evil
     and he makes him fall into his trap.
     Do all that you can
     to learn the fear of the Lord.

Grow before him like a young plant
or like a young ox becoming strong
and you will give God pleasure.
Be a man strong in word and act.
Do not make your prayer before all men like the hypocrites,
or you will end like them.   Mt 24.51
Use well every day of your existence
and in the morning think what you will offer to God that day.
Whether you are living in solitude or with others,
sit down by yourself like a wise general
and inspect your thoughts.
In short, judge yourself each day.
For it is better to be living with a thousand others
and to be humble, than to be by yourself
in a hyena's den alone with pride.
It is said about Lot
that in the midst of Sodom, a town full of sinners,
he was a good and faithful man,   2 Pet 2.8
while Cain was by himself on the earth,
with only three other people,
and we learn that he was a bad man.   see Gen 4

Watch out for the lies of the prince of Darkness

56   Now you see the struggle that is before you.
Each day think over what happened to you during the day
to examine and test,
to see if you are on our side   1 Thess 5.21
or on the side of those who fight against us.

But to you, bad spirits come from the right side
while to all other men they clearly come from the left.   *

---

* It was generally thought that bad spirits come to us from the left but good
spirits from the right.

115

Truly, they attacked me from the right, in fact.
They dragged the devil along to me
like a donkey roped for work.
But the Lord helped me.
I did not trust them.
I did not open my heart to them.
Many times I was tested by actions of the devil at my right,
and he went before me to attract my attention.

He even took his chance of testing the Lord,
but he sent him off, him and his deceits.   Mt 4.1

Happy are the poor in spirit

57   Now, my son, put on humility.   Col 3.12
Go to Christ and his good Father for their advice.
Be the friend of a man of God,
one who has the law of God in his heart.
Be like a poor man carrying his cross, and go weeping.
Let your cell be for you like the place
where Christ lay in death
till God lifts you up to see life
and gives you the crown of victory.

Be by yourself weeping before Christ

58   If a Brother causes you pain by a word ;
or if your heart wounds a Brother with the thought :
' He does not deserve to have that' ;
or if the Evil One makes the suggestion to you :
" He does not deserve that praise ",
and you agree with this thought from the devil,
and the war in your thoughts increases ;
when you have an argument with your Brother ;
keep in mind the knowledge that 'there is no balm in Gilead :
there is no doctor there.'   Jer 8.21

Without delay, look for a safe place
by yourself with God.
Be by yourself with Christ, weeping, and the Spirit of Jesus
will speak to you through your thoughts.
He will make you see how true and profound is the command :
' Love one another'.   Jn 13.34
Why fight against yourself without help
as if you are a snake with this poison in y*ou* ?

Forgive your Brother

59   Remember that you have fallen many times.
Have you not heard Christ say :
'Forgive your brother till seventy times seven.'   Mt 18.22
Have you not been many times weeping in prayer and saying :
" Forgive me for my many sins."
Now if you keep on talking about the little
that your Brother owes to you,
the Holy Spirit will at once put before your eyes
judgment and the fear of punishment for your own debt.

Happy are the peace-makers

Remember that the saints were mocked.
Look at Christ, how he was despised, cursed,
and nailed to the cross for you.
Then he will very quickly fill your heart with fear
and his mercy,
and you fall on your face weeping and saying :
" Forgive me, Lord.
I have given pain to your image."   Gen 1.26
At once you have the feeling of regret and of comfort
and you get to your feet and go quickly to your Brother
with an open heart, a happy face, a joyous mouth,
shining with peace,
and smiling at your brother you say :

" Forgive me Brother, because I gave you pain. "
You are weeping,
but a great joy comes from your weeping :
peace springs up between you
and the Spirit of God for his part shouts with joy :
" Happy are the peacemakers
for they shall be called sons of God. "   Mt 5.9
When this voice comes to the ears of the evil spirit
it covers him with shame,
glory is given to God, and you receive a great blessing.

Let us go on being faithful

60   So now, my brother, let us fight against ourselves,
     for darkness is falling on every side.
     The churches are full of people in angry argument,
     some monastic communities now desire honours,
     gold is everywhere.
     There is no one now who is a servant in love.
     No, each one crushes his neighbour.
     We have fallen into trouble and pain.
     There is no prophet and no wise man.
     Every one is hard-hearted and without feeling for others.
     Those who are wise keep quiet
     for it is an evil time.   Am 5.13
     Each one is a master to himself. They look down on others
     and act without respect.

Fight to the end to be a true monk

61   Now, my brother, be at peace with your Brother.
     Pray for me
     for I can do nothing and I am greatly troubled by my desires.
     Be watchful in everything, work hard,
     do the work of a preacher, be strong under testing.

Go on in the monastic life, fighting to the end,
taking to yourself, with humility, gentleness, and holy fear,
the wise words which you hear.
Keep your virginity.
Keep control of yourself
in your acts and in your words.
Have ever in mind the writings of the saints.

Be firm in faith in Christ Jesus our Lord.
    To him is the glory,
    to his good Father,
    and to the Holy Spirit,
for ever and ever. Amen.

Benedicite ! *

---

* 'Give blessing to God' said at the end of an instruction. Those who are
listening answer : 'Deus' : may God give us his blessing.

GLOSSARY

FEAR OF THE LORD   Mindfulness of God's holinessand care to live the common rule.   Fear of offending God is not to be confused with fear of punishment.

GREAT MONK   A mature monk who had long practised the rule and whose way of life had given him a special place within his community.

HUMILITY   Willingness to accept that we are God's creatures and dependent on him

IMAGE OF GOD   The true image of God is his only Son (Col 1.18) . God created all human beings in his image (Gen 1.27) . Therefore all are worthy of respect.

PURITY OF HEART   Singleness of purpose with a growth in simplicity ; single-mindedness, not having mixed motives. The gift of grace and the labour of a lifetime, for the Desert Fathers it was a means of growing in holiness and finding access to the kingdom of heaven..

WITNESSES FOR CHRIST SERIES

How to love – St Augustine on 1 John (extracts)
Tertullian : On Prayer
The Didache
James of Sarugh : Song about Love
St Dorotheus : Life of Dositheus
Sulpicius Severus :   St Martin of Tours
Ignatius of Antioch : Letters to Christians
Gregory the Great : Life of St Benedict

St Bernard : On the love of God
St Athanasius : Life of St Antony

WELLSPRINGS OF FAITH

A New Beginning
        Tertullian Cyril and Augustine on Baptism
Seeds of Life
        Early Christian Martyrs   (Africa and Lyons)

Life in the Spirit
   Seraphim of Sarov : Conversation with Motovilov